$\mathcal{T}$his book is a gift of love from _____

to _____ on _____

$\mathcal{I}$ want to spend time with you over the next few weeks because _____

_____

_____

_____

_____

_____

_____

_____

_____

_____

_____

_____

_____

Signature _____

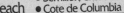

QUICK MINESTRONE SOUP

Makes 8 servings

A "homemade" soup in less than an hour! This one is very easy and flavorful.

8	ounces extra-lean ground beef or ground turkey
4	cups beef broth
1	6-ounce can low-sodium tomato paste
1	cup chopped onion
2	ribs celery, chopped
½	cup uncooked macaroni or fettuccine noodles
1	medium unpeeled potato, cut into chunks
1	16-ounce can salt-free tomatoes, including juice
1½	teaspoons dried basil
1½	teaspoons dried parsley
½	teaspoon garlic powder
1	bay leaf
½	teaspoon pepper
¼	teaspoon dried thyme
¼	teaspoon dried oregano leaves

Brown ground meat in nonstick pan, stirring constantly. Drain off any fat. In a medium saucepan combine beef with broth, tomato paste, onion, celery, macaroni, potato, tomatoes, basil, parsley, garlic powder, bay leaf, pepper, thyme and oregano. Simmer about 20 minutes or until macaroni and potatoes are tender. (Do not overcook.) Remove bay leaf before serving.

Per serving:

Calories: 192 (21% from protein, 57% from carbohydrate, 22% from fat)
Protein: 10 grams   Total fat: 5 grams   Saturated fat: 2 grams
Cholesterol: 19 mg   Sodium: 455 mg   Carbohydrate: 27 grams
Exchanges: 2 vegetable, 1 starch, 1 meat, ½ fat.

Adapted from "Tastefully Oregon"
by Oregon Dietetic Association

GROWING
LITTLE
WOMEN

GROWING LITTLE WOMEN

*Capturing Teachable
Moments with
Your Daughter*

Donna J. Miller

WITH LINDA HOLLAND

MOODY PRESS
CHICAGO

ISBN: 0-8024-2185-7

1 3 5 7 9 10 8 6 4 2

Printed in the United States of America

Linda Holland was formerly managing editor of Moody Press. Currently she serves as editorial director of Fleming H. Revell. She has three children and two grandchildren. Linda is the author of *Alabaster Doves* and coauthor of *Working Women, Workable Lives*.

To my daughters, Jennifer and Tracy,

Little did I know when God placed you in our family what a special kind of relationship could take place between a mom and daughters. I am so grateful to have you as my daughters.

Thank you for allowing me to disciple you and encourage you in beginning your walk with the Lord. That process has in turn allowed me to grow in my relationship with Him.

My prayer for both of you is Philippians 1:6: "Being confident of this, that he who began a good work in you will carry it on to completion until the day of Christ Jesus." Spending this time with each of you brought some of the best moments of my life.

I love you as big as the whole world!

Mom

To my husband, Don,

You have always been the support and loving husband I needed. Thank you for your encouragement to spend this special time with our daughters. I love being your wife and partner in ministry.

Lovingly,

Donna

CONTENTS

Section One
You're a Character!

Section Two
Happily Ever After . . .

Section Three
Gifts from the Heart

Section Four
Commitment Is Cool

ACKNOWLEDGMENTS

*W*hen I began collecting information ten years ago to disciple my daughters, I never dreamed these materials would be published for other moms to use with their children. I am so thankful to the Lord for giving me the idea to disciple my daughters and then bringing key people into my life to make this book possible.

I am very grateful to the following people for their contributions and the way they helped me in this project.

- To Ron and Mary Bennett and Jim and Becky Sorensen, thank you for your love of one-on-one discipleship, which proved to be the setting for the Lord to speak to me.
- To my parents, Henri and Thelma Caquelard, and my sisters, Suzi and Runa, for your love, support, and prayers.
- To Ronda, Catherine, and Lorrie, my three very special friends who hold a dear place in my heart. I can never repay you for your sacrifice of time and your encouragement to keep me on task. Without you this book would not have become a reality.
- To my prayer partner, Kathy Chesney, for her love and support and interest in this project.
- To Linda Holland, for realizing there is a need for mothers to mentor their daughters and for your knowledge and expertise. I am thankful.

Dear Mothers,

In 1985 my husband and I started meeting with a small group in our church to study a course on lifestyle evangelism. It was especially challenging and exciting for me as I learned how to discuss my faith in a nonthreatening way with unbelievers. At the end of this course, we were all assigned to target three or four people to witness our Christian faith to. If we were able to lead them to Christ, we were to disciple them afterward.

During the next few weeks, I asked the Lord to lead me to the right people and to prepare their hearts to receive Him. Each time I prayed, my older daughter, Jennifer, came to mind. I kept praying.

After a few weeks, I finally got the hint. The toughest challenge of all—to disciple one of my own children. I immediately began collecting resources and ideas to use in my discipling with Jennifer. A few years later I discipled my younger daughter, Tracy.

How I would love to sit down with each of you and tell you what the months of discipling my daughters have meant to me. Even though the active time of discipling is now over, I can still see the positive effects it had on each of us. It is clear to me that the time we spent together in those formative years strengthened our relationships in their teenage years. Our time together bonded us to each other and laid a foundation of open communication, helping us establish mutual trust and loyalty that grew into a warm, lasting friendship.

As a mother, it is very important that you first examine your own heart before you begin discipling your daughter. I encourage you to be absolutely certain that you have a personal relationship with Jesus Christ and know Him personally as your Savior and Lord. If you are not sure whether or not you know Him or you don't know what I mean, I am asking whether you have ever told God you know you're a sinner, you can't save yourself, and you accept Jesus Christ's death on the cross as the payment and forgiveness of your sins. (See John 3:16.)

Chapter 10 has a chance for you to ask your daughter if she has ever made this most important decision. If she has not done so, you may want to wait until later to go through this book with her or use that chapter an earlier week. Even if you are quite sure of her standing with God, ask her to articulate answers to the questions in chapter 10.

As the mom, you will set the tone for your time together, so be relaxed and expect to have fun! There is no right or wrong way to go about it. The important thing is not whether or not you complete a chapter each week. The goal is for you and your daughter to get to know each other better and for you to share a part of yourself with your daughter. The time you spend together is an investment in developing her character and instilling meaningful values. The result is that the two of you will grow together as you learn more about the Lord.

My daughters will not be perfect because of our time together, but I have already seen the Lord use what they learned in many ways. My prayer is that you and your daughter will grow together in the Lord and in your friendship.

She will probably never be the same again . . . and neither will you.

Donna Miller

Dear Daughters,

I was privileged to be the first in our family to experience this special time with my mom. During my sixth grade year, my mom and I spent time together each week. This was a special time in my life. What I didn't understand, my mom explained to me. I have already been able many times to use the lessons I learned.

As someone who has gone through this experience, I can assure you that it was a wonderful time for both of us. We looked forward to our time every week. You also will enjoy becoming closer to your mom while having fun and learning more about God's Word.

Many of the things I learned have stayed with me throughout high school. In fact, I think I'll carry them all of my life. My mom has always encouraged me to share my faith in Christ. Being in public school gave me many opportunities to do that. That's why I have chosen Matthew 5:13–16 as my life verses:

> You are the salt of the earth. But if the salt loses its saltiness, how can it be made salty again? It is no longer good for anything, except to be thrown out and trampled by men. You are the light of the world. A city on a hill cannot be hidden. Neither do people light a lamp and put it under a bowl. Instead they put it on its stand, and it gives light to everyone in the house. In the same way, let your light shine before men, that they may see your good deeds and praise your Father in heaven.

My mom and I have a wonderful relationship that has grown into a special friendship over the years. One of the reasons is because my mom took time out of her busy schedule to be with *just me!* So, give this idea a chance. You'll take away from this time together many great memories and the foundation for a great future.

Love in Christ,

Jennifer Miller

BEING YOUR DAUGHTER'S MENTOR

DEFINITION OF A MENTOR:
A trusted counselor or guide; wise and trusted adviser.

The apostle Paul was not afraid to say, "Follow my example, as I follow the example of Christ" (1 Corinthians 11:1).

Our daughters are following us. As they follow us, what will they see? In our own lives let's offer our daughters an image of Philippians 4:8: "Whatever is true, whatever is noble, whatever is right, whatever is pure, whatever is lovely, whatever is admirable—if anything is excellent or praiseworthy—think about such things."

WHY DO WE MEET?

- so my daughter and I will get to know each other better; to spend special time together one-on-one; and to share my values with her.
- so my daughter will gain more insight about her identity in Christ and begin to think about her future. I'll try to answer her questions about her Christian walk and why we believe as we do.
- so that each of us will learn more about the Lord and grow spiritually.
- to build her character for the future.
- so that our relationship will grow stronger and I can show her how much I love her.

HOW TO USE THIS BOOK

*F*irst of all, you need to begin praying for the time when you will be discipling your daughter. Then, little by little, introduce the idea to her. Don't just *announce* your plan. *Ask* her how she feels about getting together once a week for a special time just between the two of you. It is important that she looks forward to doing this with you.

Mom, you will set the tone for your time together. If you are excited and enthusiastic about the idea, she will likely feel the same way about it. So remember:

Be fun!

Be creative!

Be committed!

The lessons are approximately an hour long and meant to be used for sixteen consecutive weeks. Some weeks include additional activities (called "action ideas") that can be done at a separate time during the week or even saved for a later date. Some of these apply the lessons of the week; some are just ideas of ways you and your daughter can spend time together.

Plan to begin at a time when you will be able to follow through each week. Choose a time when pressures at home are reduced. For some that might be summertime; for others, after school begins in the fall. But pick a time when you're less likely to be running a family of kids to little league or music lessons or somewhere else. Schedule this hour into your week and make it a priority, or it simply won't happen on a regular basis.

Plan ahead. Resist the temptation to just sit down and begin the lessons. Read through or at least scan the chapters to get an idea where you're headed in this adventure. The important thing is to think through the materials and be comfortable with them before you start.

Each chapter begins with a Scripture reading to get you

thinking about the topic, then a short story relating to the theme for that week. These stories are designed for you to read aloud to your daughter. It may have been a while since you've read a story to her, but reading to her will nurture her soul. Don't underestimate the impact this will make on your success.

Try to make time to read the story in advance of your meeting time so that you will be familiar with it. Then read it aloud with inflection and lots of drama. Your daughter will love this special attention you give her. And this will give you a chance to savor the last fleeting moments of her childhood. If she insists she is too old to have you read to her, have her read the story to you, take turns reading, or obtain two copies of the book and read them silently but in the same room.

Once you've read the story, read and discuss the questions that follow. These three or four questions will help to get both of you talking about the story and subject for the week. Then hand the book to your daughter and help her look up verses while she fills in the blanks in "What Does the Bible Say?" Notice that the version I have used is the NIV; it will be easier to know what goes in each blank if you use the same version. All of this leads us to the heart of the book—discussing and applying these scriptural truths to your daughter's life today. This section of the book is where you will become closer to your daughter as each of you tells your thoughts. We've provided space for you to document your discussion. This section is called "Looking Deeper." Some questions are mainly for the mother, some for the daughter, and some for both of you. (Those for both are labeled "for discussion." But actually, all three categories are for discussion.)

In the process, you'll come to better understand your daughter, while at the same time passing on to her timeless principles. Personalizing the book will give her a keepsake of your time together. Each chapter closes with a memory verse for the week and a prayer.

One way this book will be personalized is by your own stories, experience, wisdom, and knowledge of your daughter. Many of these sessions will probably be intimate hours for the two of you. And she may ask you some very good questions you could have a hard time answering. What if your younger years included some indiscretion or even rebellion toward God? How will you deal with that without giving the impression either that "What I did was sin, but it sure was exciting" or "I dabbled in sin, but I turned out OK"? Think through what you will say. You might want to tell her something like this, "When I was young, I made some choices that were not very smart and that were sinful. I didn't know Christ as my Savior [or: I chose to put myself first, before God]. Christ has changed my life tremendously, but I've paid for the choices I made, and I'd like to spare you that pain. If I knew then what I know now, I would have made different choices. This is not a 'cop-out'; I simply want what's best for you. I don't want you to have to learn this the hard way, like I did."

Chapter 16 may be the most important chapter in the book. It is your chapter to personalize—filled with a lot of blank spaces designed to give you a chance to tell your daughter a story of your own. That might be a story about the day she was born or how you met and fell in love with her father. You may choose to tell her how you came to know and accept Christ. We've titled this chapter "A Gift from Mom's Heart," because this truly is the best gift you can give your daughter—a piece of your own heart and a chance to celebrate and mark the closing of your special time together.

Other places that need your personal touch include the presentation page (in the front) and the certificate of commitment (in the back). The first is a personal note from you to your daughter; the second is a commitment that the two of you will make together if you desire. It could be the commitment to meet together during this time, or it could be a commitment that extends beyond that time—perhaps some way to stay in touch with each other's lives, or even a promise to practice sexual purity. It's up to the two of you.

We have attempted to craft this book for girls between the ages of nine and twelve. But girls develop in varying stages during these years. You know your daughter best and understand her emotional and spiritual development. For this reason, we ask you to read through each week before engaging in it with your daughter. If you feel she is not yet ready to deal with the concepts or subject matter in any particular chapter, skip past it to another. In fact, feel free to skip around or change the sequence of topics as you feel necessary to make your time with her special.

The important thing is that this time bonds you together with warm moments worth keeping and celebrating. As your daughter approaches her teenage years, there is no better time for you to capture teachable moments with her. These preteen years allow you an opportunity to observe your daughter's dawn of womanhood. And you will be there to listen and offer support.

You'll never regret the time you've carved out to be together . . . and neither will your daughter.

Section One

YOU'RE A CHARACTER!

Week One

A DOVE IN GOD'S GARDEN

Scripture Reading for This Week

Matthew 10:29–31
Are not two sparrows sold for a penny? Yet not one of them will fall to the ground apart from the will of your Father. And even the very hairs of your head are all numbered. So don't be afraid; you are worth more than many sparrows.

What words best describe the main point of this passage? Write them in the space below.

*Daughter*_____

Mom _____

Psalm 139:13–16
For you created my inmost being; you knit me together in my mother's womb. I praise you because I am fearfully and wonderfully made; . . . My frame was not hidden from you when I was made in the secret place. When I was woven together in the

depths of the earth, your eyes saw my unformed body. All the days ordained for me were written in your book before one of them came to be.

What words best describe the main point of these verses? Write them in the space below.

*Daughter*_____

Mom   _____

Tell each other why you chose these words.

*A*s dawn birthed the morning of the sixth day of creation, God stood back and inspected His work.

The sun in the sky cast its warmth over rolling grassy hills and majestic mountains that jutted up between the valleys and plains of earth, pointing back toward heaven. Birds of every kind soared the azure skies before returning to their nests on the seashore or land. Animals of every species found homes in their favorite terrain, while fish and dolphins and other creatures swam vast oceans, lakes, and rivers.

A lazy river meandered through the Garden of Eden where God had placed the first man, Adam, to live. At nightfall the river swelled until it spilled over its banks and blanketed the garden with a thin sheet of water that nourished the lush foliage. As the sun burst on each new day, the water receded, leaving a covering of dew on the ground.

God came down from heaven and walked through the sleeping garden looking for Adam. The power of His presence stirred a breeze that rustled leaves in a whisper of praise to the Mighty Creator.

God found Adam sleeping in a patch of moss growing in the hollowed-out trunk of a redwood tree. For a few moments, God just stood and watched Adam's chest rise and fall to the rhythm of his restful breath. God took pleasure in what He had created. It was good. But He had not yet finished His work. To be complete, earth required one final touch of the Creator's hands.

While Adam slept, God reached His hand down and took one of his ribs, closing up the flesh around it. Stooping near the ground, He gently laid the rib in the soil in front of Him. His hands scooped soft, moist dirt and heaped it in a mound over the bone. Then those powerful yet gentle hands molded and shaped a new creation.

As God worked, the creature gradually began to take shape. The form looked a lot like Adam, but at the same time distinctly different. This image was smaller and rounder than Adam and had a softer appearance.

Several animals poked their curious faces through the bushes to get a better look. They watched . . . wondering. A bear padded boldly right up to the creature and sniffed. Other animals began to creep closer now, fascinated by this new addition to the garden.

God paused briefly, considering the qualities this new creation would require to fulfill her purpose on earth.

Overhead, a dove cut against the wind, striking a fanciful silhouette against the blue. God watched the bird rise higher and higher into the sky, pumping its wings harder, faster, higher until it was merely a speck in the heavens. God bid the bird to come to Him, and the pale speck in the distance grew bigger and bigger as the dove suddenly plunged toward earth. Dropping near the ground, it spread its wings and glided to rest on God's shoulder.

God whispered softly to the dove and stroked the back of its head as it cooed its allegiance to the Mighty Creator. He loved the qualities of the dove—gentle, friendly, and delicate. To Him the dove represented peacefulness, loyalty, and purity.

Inside woman, God placed the gentle characteristics of the dove.

But like Adam, this new creation would also need to be strong like the lion. But, no, not the lion. More like the strength of the alabaster—a pure, white stone God had tucked into the hillsides of Milan. Yes, that was more like it—strong, yet beautiful and translucent.

Now the creature was complete.

God smiled. Then, inhaling deeply, He breathed life into the woman.

Once more, God viewed His masterpiece. "It is perfect," He said with a smile as He woke Adam up to make the introduction.

Adam was clearly delighted. "I will call you Eve," he said to her. Then God rested from His work.

What the Story Says

We are God's pride and joy. As our Creator, He knows us well and delights in our unique characteristics.

Discussion Questions

1. What does it mean when we say that God delights in us?

2. Have you ever made something that gave you pleasure? Do you think that might be how God felt?

3. Do you think God delights in your unique traits—those qualities that make you different from anyone else?

DEFINITION OF DELIGHT:
   To take great pleasure, joy, and satisfaction.

DEFINITION OF UNIQUE:
   Distinct, one of a kind.

What Does the Bible Say?

Look up the following Scriptures and fill in the blanks.

Psalm 149:4
For the Lord takes _____ in his _____.

Psalm 103:14
For he _____ how we are _____.

What does this tell you about the level of God's involvement in our personal lives?

Matthew 10:30
And even the very _____ of your head are all _____
_____.

If God knows even the small details about us, how much more does He care about the more important things in our lives?

Zephaniah 3:17
The Lord your God is _____ _____ , he is _____
_____ _____. He will take great delight in you, he will quiet you with his love, he will rejoice over you with singing.

Look at the second part of the last verse. It says, "He will take great delight in you . . . he will rejoice over you with singing."
Write one word that best describes how that makes you feel.

*Daughter*_____

Mom _____

_____

Looking Deeper

For Discussion:

Ask each other to list some of the qualities that make each of you unique.

Daughter:

_____

_____

_____

_____

Mom:

_____

_____

_____

_____

Together, list three ways you can begin to use those qualities on a daily basis.

1. _____

2. _____

3. _____

List three things both of you could do this week that would please God.

1. _____

2. _____

3. _____

Compare your ideas with these:

- Go to bed early one night each week to enjoy a leisurely chat with God.
- Read from your Bible every day, even if all you can manage is a few verses.

- Ask God each morning to accompany you throughout your day.

Wow! Now you have six great ideas. Practice them this week.

For Discussion:

Discuss and list below three reasons you know you are special to God.

1. _____

2. _____

3. _____

Compare your ideas with these:

- His Word says so.
- He died on the cross for my sins.
- I experience His love when I feel His presence.

Action Ideas

Spend some time looking at old photos of you and your family. Daughter, ask your mother to tell you all about the day you were born.

Words to Memorize

For the Lord takes delight in his people.
Psalm 149:4

Your Goal for This Week

_____

_____

_____

Closing Prayer

Lord, help me to remember that You created me for Your pleasure. Teach me how to please You in all that I do.

Week Two

A Heart That's Pure

Scripture Reading for This Week

Luke 1:46–55
And Mary said: "My soul glorifies the Lord and my spirit rejoices in God my Savior, for he has been mindful of the humble state of his servant. From now on all generations will call me blessed, for the Mighty One has done great things for me—holy is his name. His mercy extends to those who fear him, from generation to generation. He has performed mighty deeds with his arm; he has scattered those who are proud in their inmost thoughts. He has brought down rulers from their thrones but has lifted up the humble. He has filled the hungry with good things but has sent the rich away empty. He has helped his servant Israel, remembering to be merciful to Abraham and his descendants forever, even as he said to our fathers."

What words best describe the main point of these verses? Write them in the space below.

*Daughter*_____

_____

Tell each other why you chose these words.

*O*n the streets of heaven, the changing of the guard caused a windstorm of activity as some angels returned from their earthly assignments and others left to take the next shift. Those returning stopped at the Streets of Gold Newsstand to pick up the evening edition of the *Celestial Tribune.* A flame of excitement ignited the air, spreading like wildfire in the wind as, one by one, the heavenly hosts noticed the day's headline. It said: "Messiah to Be Born." And just below that: "Tonight God's Son Becomes a Child."

Awed by the significance of this long-awaited occurrence, the celestials whispered among themselves, "Today's the day! Today's the day!" They chattered and nodded to one another as they read the article that followed. The news column announced that God's commanding officer—the archangel Gabriel—had played a significant role in the event. All were invited to attend a meeting to celebrate.

In the center of the city, a majestic crystal palace rose from the golden streets, perched atop a platinum scaffold like a gigantic diamond solitaire. It sparkled, its facets casting prisms of color over the terrain. The Architect had left the roof of this structure open to allow for a panoramic view of the universe.

The celestials converged now on the great hall, where God convened the meeting with Gabriel at attention before Him. Divine love traced the Sovereign's face as He reminded them all of His perfect plan to ransom His wayward children.

When God paused, Gabriel approached the throne. His expression revealed his excitement as he looked into God's eyes and asked, "Master, can it be true? Is tonight really the night?"

"It is true!" God confirmed. "The time has come. Tonight My Beloved Son will be born as a child to save My people from their sins."

Gabriel tilted his head slightly to one side as he listened

earnestly to God's every word. He knew well his assignment, for he had rehearsed his part in this plan since the beginning of time.

The Almighty stood to His feet, opening His arms in a grand, sweeping gesture. The glory of His presence electrified the atmosphere as all of heaven waited, listening attentively for the voice of their God.

Finally, He spoke. "I have searched the earth for a special young woman to be My servant. Not a stranger. Someone familiar to Me. Someone pure. Someone I can trust with the life of My one and only Son." A wistfulness settled on God's face as He spoke of His Son.

"I have chosen a girl named Mary," God continued. "She is a descendant of my servant David. I know her well because she worships Me with her whole heart. In all the world there is none with a heart so pure as Mary's. I can trust Mary with My Son. Tonight she will give birth to Him and name Him Jesus."

As God spoke and angels watched, Gabriel's wings fluttered behind him anticipating his departure. And heaven poised breathlessly, marking the moment that would alter the destiny of the world forever.

"I know exactly what to do." Gabriel bowed his allegiance, and with the reverberating sound of a thousand birds in flight, he spread his massive wings and ascended high above heaven. Then, tucking his wings close to his body, he plunged suddenly out of sight toward earth to announce the special gift God had sent to earth.

❄ ❄ ❄

Several months earlier, starlight fell from a midnight sky across the sleeping town of Nazareth. All was quiet except for the lowing of cattle that stirred in the pastures and an occasional rustling of leaves tossed about by a warm breeze. On the edge of town, in a mud-walled hovel, a girl lay in deep slumber on a mat. Her long, dark hair fell away from skin tanned from long days spent under the fierce eastern sun.

Because she was now in her teens, Jewish culture considered Mary a young woman; she was ready to marry and begin her own family. Mary was fortunate. Her father had promised her in marriage to a kind and gentle carpenter named Joseph, who Mary thought was the finest young man in all of Galilee. Over time, she had grown to love him deeply.

As Mary slept, visions of her upcoming wedding danced happily in her dreams.

Suddenly, a flash of light burst through the doorway, illuminating even the shadowy corners of the room. Startled awake, Mary bolted upright in her bed. Her hands flew up instinctively to shield her eyes from the glare as she squinted blindly at a form that now began to take shape on the threshold. She rubbed her groggy eyes briskly with her fists, attempting to wake herself from this terrible nightmare, but when she looked again, the creature was still there.

As her eyes began to adjust to the light, Mary could see a brilliant image standing in the doorway. He wore a shimmering robe that spilled over his feet and onto the floor. Two glistening wings rested against his massive shoulders, extending down his back and brushing the floor. His long hair framed a striking face that seemed to radiate the presence of God.

Terrified and still squinting, Mary sprang to her feet and crouched against the cold wall.

"Don't be afraid, Mary. My name is Gabriel, and I've come to congratulate you." The angel's voice echoed in Mary's head. "The Lord takes great pleasure in you, because you worship and love Him completely."

Mary froze, her hands clutching her robe. The pounding of her heartbeat raced in her ears, and a lump formed in her throat.

"There is no reason to be afraid, Mary," Gabriel comforted her. "God is going to bless you in a wonderful way!"

Mary straightened slightly, but confusion etched her face as she struggled to make sense of the angel's words.

"Very soon now," Gabriel spoke gently, "you will become pregnant and give birth to a baby boy. This baby is the Son of

God—the Messiah that God has promised!" Gabriel stepped forward and looked into Mary's eyes. "Name Him Jesus," he said slowly to be sure she understood him. "As it was written, God will give His Son the throne of His ancestor David, and He will reign over Israel forever."

Mary swallowed hard and then swallowed hard again, trying to reclaim her voice. "B-b-but . . . how can I have a baby?" she whispered. "I'm . . . I'm a virgin."

"Don't worry, Mary," Gabriel assured her. "You will become pregnant by the Holy Spirit and God's power."

Mary stared intently into the angel's eyes, no longer afraid as she felt a strange peace pour over her like warm oil. "I am the Lord's servant," a more confident Mary spoke now. "I am willing to do whatever He asks. Let everything you have said come true."

As the last syllable escaped Mary's lips, the angel simply disappeared, and Mary stood alone in the dark. No fanfare. Not even a glow left behind to mark the event. Just complete silence.

Back in heaven, God smiled as He viewed the scene in Nazareth and awaited Gabriel's return. He didn't have to wait long, for Gabriel suddenly appeared before Him, and all of heaven sprang into a celebration of praise to the Son of God.

Beaming like a proud Father, God reached His hand high into the heavens, chose the brightest star, and plucked it from the universe. With a sweep of His hand, He flung the star into the eastern sky, setting it on a course that would one day guide wisemen to a tiny stable in Bethlehem, where a feed box for barnyard animals cradled the Savior of the world.

What the Story Says

God uses young women who will keep
themselves pure and serve Him wholeheartedly.

Discussion Questions

1. What do you think it means to be pure of heart?
2. What does it mean to serve God wholeheartedly?
3. How can a young woman be pure today?

DEFINITION OF PURITY:
> Containing nothing that does not belong; free from moral fault or guilt; pure in conduct and intention.

What Does the Bible Say?

Look up the following Scriptures and fill in the blanks.

1 Timothy 4:12
Don't let anyone look down on you because you are young, but set an example for the believers in speech, in life, in love, in faith and in _____.

How can you "set an example"?

1 Timothy 5:1–2
Do not rebuke an older man harshly, but _____ him as if he were your father. Treat younger men as _____, older women as mothers, and younger women as _____, with absolute purity.

What does it mean to "exhort"?

Does this mean that God expects purity in all of our relationships?

Psalm 51:10–11
Create in me a _____,
O God, and renew a steadfast spirit within me. Do not cast me
from your _____ or take your Holy
Spirit from me.

Word Scramble

1. ewren _____
2. ruytpi _____
3. atsfedats _____

(For answers to this and other word scrambles, see page
196.)

Looking Deeper

For Discussion:

List several qualities that come to mind when you think of purity.

_____

_____

_____

Compare your list of qualities to the list below:

- Loves God
- Speaks the truth
- Guards her thoughts
- Practices chastity
- Speaks kindly
- Can be trusted
- Keeps her promises

Discuss and then define each of the following qualities:

Honesty _____

Trustworthiness _____

Chastity _____

Honor _____

For Mom:

Tell your daughter which of these qualities is the most difficult for you to maintain. Write it below and tell why.

_____

_____

_____

Tell your daughter what has helped you in your struggle to overcome this challenge. Write it below.

_____

_____

_____

Discuss with your daughter some ways she can guard her purity over the coming years. Point out that Mary was pure before God, but her actions before people were also pure. Some elements in the discussion (not lecture) may include:

For Discussion:

1. Why does it matter what a young woman wears?
2. Why do you feel it wise to limit what your daughter sees on television or at the movies and what she reads?

3. What are appropriate ways to respond to a young man? This could include femininity, social skills, and physical conduct with:

   a. boys in general

   b. a boy she is interested in (flirting)

   c. one she is dating

   d. one she is engaged to

4. How does a young woman keep her thoughts pure?

5. How permanent did God intend marriage to be? Is marriage a plan, a promise, a commitment, or a covenant? What's the difference?

For Mom:

When you look ahead to the next few years, what are some of the possible challenges your daughter may face in her efforts to be pure and serve God wholeheartedly? Discuss your thoughts and hers, and list them below.

_____

_____

_____

For Discussion:

Together, compare your list to these possibilities:

- She could become so busy with school and friends that she neglects her time alone with God.
- Her priorities may change so that God will no longer hold the number one place in her heart.
- She probably will feel pressure to behave like her non-Christian friends.

For Mom:

Discuss and identify three God-given qualities your daughter possesses that will help her maintain purity. Write them below.

1. _____
2. _____
3. _____

How can she develop these qualities on a daily basis?

_____

_____

_____

For Daughter:

List several things you can do today to keep your heart pure.

_____

_____

_____

_____

Compare your ideas with these:

- Confess your sins and ask for forgiveness.
- Ask for God's help.
- Read your Bible.
- Model your behavior after Christ's
- Listen to your conscience.

6. Think before you act.

Great! Now you have a plan. Try practicing these ideas this week.

For Discussion:

Discuss your ideas and list three ways God can use a young woman who is pure and wants to serve Him.

1. _____
2. _____
3. _____

Action Ideas

Set up a time to meet with a high school or college girl who is a Christian and is leading a life of purity because of what Christ means to her. What has given her the strength to do the right things?

Words to Memorize

Create in me a pure heart, O God.
Psalm 51:10

Your Goal for This Week

_____

_____

_____

Closing Prayer

Lord, give me a heart that is pure.

Week Three

DANGEROUS COMPANY

Scripture Reading for This Week

1 Corinthians 5:11
But now I am writing you that you must not associate with anyone who calls himself a brother but is sexually immoral or
greedy, an idolater or a slanderer, a drunkard or a swindler. With
such a man do not even eat.

What does it mean to "associate" with someone?

Galatians 6:9
Let us not become weary in doing good, for at the proper time
we will reap a harvest if we do not give up.

Psalm 1:1
Blessed is the man who does not walk in the counsel of the wicked
or stand in the way of sinners or sit in the seat of mockers.

What words best describe the main point of these verses? Write
them in the space below.

Daughter _____

Mom _____

Tell each other why you chose these words.

*J*oni Williams saddled up her mare Mazy, then placed her left boot in the stirrup and swung herself up into the saddle. Tugging hard on the reins, she turned Mazy away from the barn and headed into the front yard. As she crossed the yard, she waved good-bye toward the porch where her mother stood. "I'll be back in a couple hours," Joni called.

"Now don't be late for dinner," her mother hollered, waving back.

"I won't, Mama," Joni promised, then trotted Mazy around to the back lot of her family's ranch house and carefully guided her across the shallow creek that divided their backyard from the grasslands. Again on dry land, she tapped her heels against the mare's flanks, prompting her to a full gallop over the golden pastures that seemed to stretch endlessly across the Texas range.

Joni's black braids bounced against her back, rising and falling in time with Mazy's rhythmic gait. She loved the exhilaration of riding Mazy hard and fast. Loved the feeling of power beneath her as the mare pushed the limits of her strength. Loved the blast of wind against her dark brown skin and the sight of Mazy's amber mane dancing upon it.

And Joni loved Mazy.

Every Saturday afternoon, weather permitting, Joni met her neighbor and best friend, Melissa, halfway between their ranches to ride for a while. A happy ritual had developed. Joni looked forward to these adventurous distractions because ranch life could sometimes be lonely, and Melissa was always lots of fun to hang out with.

Joni hunkered low against Mazy's withers and raced on toward her rendezvous with Melissa. Before long, she could see a tiny dot skimming the horizon in the distance and growing steadily larger. Within minutes, Melissa was in plain view, hunkered low like Joni and approaching fast.

Just short of passing each other, both girls pulled back firmly on their reins and stopped their mounts suddenly, stirring the dust in billows around their dancing hooves.

Melissa couldn't wait to blurt out, "Guess where we're going?" She panted and smiled, showing a full set of teeth with braces.

"Where?" Joni's curiosity rose to the occasion.

"Kurt Ferris called just as I was leaving. He wants us to come over to his house this afternoon." Melissa beamed at Joni. "You know, dreamy-eyes Kurt Ferris? Like Kurt, the most popular guy in eighth grade! Can you believe it?" she squealed. "He said he saw you last week in town and you are looking s-o-o-o-o good," Melissa drawled. "Isn't that hysterical?"

They both laughed, but Joni felt a blush cross her face. The blush came from a carefully nurtured crush that had begun when they were kids and raised lambs together in 4H. But since Joni was a year younger than Kurt, he had never paid her much attention.

Joni still thought about Kurt, though.

"Isn't Kurt going out with Amy?" Joni asked Melissa.

"They broke up."

"What'll I say to him?" Joni gave Melissa a quizzical look.

"Just say 'hi' and smile a lot," Melissa offered her advice.

"So, what are we waiting for?" Joni quipped as she pulled the reins to her right, turning Mazy around. "I'll race you there!" she called over her shoulder as she dug her heels into Mazy and headed toward the Ferris ranch with Melissa close behind.

As they approached the Ferris yard, loud music and laughter greeted them from the house. The girls hitched their horses to a post outside the barn, then walked to the front door and rang the bell.

No answer.

They rang again and rapped loudly with the door knocker.

At last the door swung open and Kurt stood there, mischief in his eyes, an enormous grin on his face. "C'mon in," he slurred. "We're all hangin' out in the living room." He opened the door wider and bowed low, sweeping his arm in a welcoming gesture. He had obviously been drinking.

"Hi, Kurt," both girls chimed together as they stepped into the foyer and stood looking at the cutest guy in the county.

Kurt slipped his arm through Joni's and managed to escort her and Melissa across the foyer and into the living room. Joni could smell alcohol on his breath. It made her feel queasy.

"You guys know everybody here, don't you?" Kurt motioned toward the living room.

"Sure," Melissa lied.

"Go on in and I'll get you something to drink." He grinned and left them.

The living room swarmed with a dozen or so kids from school—the most popular group at Central Middle School. Several kids huddled in the center. A few of them held cigarettes between their fingers, occasionally lifting them to their lips to take short, awkward drags before blowing out a haze of smoke that hovered like gray clouds above their heads. A few more kids were scattered on the patio sipping from clear plastic cups that Joni suspected contained more than soda, because on the coffee table among the soda cans stood a half-empty bottle of alcohol and several beer cans.

Melissa marched right up to one group, leaving Joni standing in the entrance alone. Joni watched for a moment, impressed with how instinctively Melissa fit in with the others. Feeling awkward just standing there, she plopped down in an easy chair on one side of the room and gawked around.

Within seconds Kurt had returned. Squatting to eye level, he shoved a plastic cup in her hand so hard that the contents almost splashed into her lap. Lifting his own glass, he proposed a toast. "To love and friendship and the most beautiful girl in school." He tapped the rim of his cup against Joni's and then took a sip.

"What's in this?" Joni glanced at the cup in her hand.

"It's really good. You'll like it." Kurt sidestepped her question.

"What's in it?" Joni repeated.

"Just a little rum and Coke," Kurt flashed his most engaging smile. "C'mon, join the party," Kurt's eyes threatened to melt Joni in a puddle on the floor.

"I guess a little won't hurt."

"Look, Joni, let's get away from the crowd. I want to spend some time with you alone. I've got to talk to someone. You think about it, and I'll be back in a minute." He stood up and stumbled out of the room.

Joni just sat and stared at the cup in her hand. She could smell the pungent odor of alcohol. She felt a pang of guilt as she remembered smelling that same odor on her sister's breath last summer after she had fallen from her horse and broken her arm. Mama had said she was lucky she hadn't broken her neck, and then Mama had a long talk with her girls about the hazards of alcohol and drugs. Then she gave each of them a book to read on the topic and followed up with a discussion of what they had learned.

"Hey, Joni, isn't this great?" Melissa's voice jolted her back to the present.

"Melissa." Joni grabbed her arm. "I need to talk to you."

"What's wrong?" Melissa asked.

"I don't think we should be here. I want to go."

"Joni," Melissa pleaded, "this is the first time we've been invited to party with the most popular group in school. Don't spoil it." Melissa looked over her shoulder to see what the others were doing in her absence. "Besides, Kurt is crazy about you. Just relax. We'll leave in a little while . . . OK?" Melissa rejoined the others.

When Kurt didn't return after several minutes, Joni decided to go in search of the bathroom. She walked to the opposite side of the living room, through the dining room, and into the hallway. Suddenly, she recognized Kurt standing with his back to her at the end of the hallway. He was talking to Amy.

"Look, Amy, we just need to spend some time alone . . ."

Joni let out a tiny gasp. She turned an immediate about-face and headed back into the living room to find Melissa. She found her sitting on a lower step of the stairs.

"Melissa, Kurt's getting back together with Amy," Joni confided in her friend.

"Forget about Kurt. He's not worth it. Anyway, Joni, look around you. As they say, 'there's plenty of other fish in the sea.' "

Joni just stood and stared down at Melissa as anger swelled in her throat.

But Melissa couldn't leave bad enough alone. She added, "You're not going to run home like a little baby, are you?"

That was it for Joni. She turned abruptly and walked away, and she didn't stop until she reached the post by the barn where Mazy waited patiently. She untied her horse and nuzzled her cheek against Mazy's velvety muzzle as she stroked the sides of her face. "Good girl. Good girl," Joni crooned to her beloved mare. "Let's go home."

Joni swung herself up into the saddle and walked Mazy out of the yard. Once in open range, Joni gave a gentle nudge to the horse's flanks. The horse responded, breaking into an easy gallop as Joni hovered low and tried to race the wind back home.

What the Story Says

Flee from evil. When friends lead you
into trouble, you need to change your friends.

Discussion Questions

1. What good decisions did Joni make?

2. What would you do if you found yourself in a similar situation?

3. What would you do if you wanted to leave, but didn't have a ride home? Ask your mom what she would do.

4. What dangers did Joni encounter? What might have happened?

DEFINITION OF PEER:
   One belonging to the same age, grade, or status.

DEFINITION OF PRESSURE:
   Physical or mental distress.

What Does the Bible Say?

Look up the following Scriptures and fill in the blanks.

Exodus 23:2
Do not _____ the crowd in doing wrong. When you give testimony in a lawsuit, do not pervert justice by _____ with the crowd.

1 Corinthians 15:33
Do not be misled: _____
corrupts good character.

What does it mean to corrupt good character?

Proverbs 24:1
Do not _____ wicked men, do not _____ their company.

Ephesians 5:15
Be very careful, then, how you live—not as_____ but as_____.

Proverbs 13:20
He who walks with the_____ grows wise, but a
companion of fools suffers _____.

*What kind of harm might come from hanging around with the
wrong company?*

Looking Deeper

For Discussion:

What are some of the traits you look for in a good friend?

_____

_____

_____

Compare your list to the following possibilities:

> **W** isdom
> **I** ntegrity
> **S** incerity
> **E** ncouragement

In what ways can friends enrich our lives?

_____

_____

_____

What are some of the sacrifices we may be called upon to make
as friends?

_____

_____

Compare your list to the following possibilities:

- To stand up for your friend when she is being treated badly.
- To defend her when others talk about her.
- To be supportive when your friend needs advice or encouragement.

In what ways might the wrong friends lead you into trouble? List a few possibilities below.

_____

_____

_____

Compare your list to these possibilities:

- They may encourage you to lie to your parents about where you're going and what you're doing. If you feel you have to lie, there's probably something wrong with what you're doing.
- They may offer you alcohol, cigarettes, or even illegal drugs. Can you resist this pressure even if your friends don't?
- Some of your friends who don't understand your love for Christ may make fun of your faith. Will you still be proud to be called a Christian?

For Mom:

Discuss and identify three God-given strengths your daughter possesses that will help her resist peer pressure. Write them below.

1. _____

2. _____

3. _____

How can she develop these strengths on a daily basis? List two ways here.

1. _____

2. _____

For Daughter:

Discuss with your mom, then list below, three steps you can take to prepare for peer pressure.

1. _____

2. _____

3. _____

Compare your ideas with those below.

- You and your mom can rehearse ways to respond to particular situations before they arise.
- You could practice saying, "No!" Say it over and over again until you feel comfortable with it.
- Each day tell your problems to the Lord and ask for His guidance and wisdom.

Super! Now you have a plan. Role play it again later this week.

For Discussion:

Discuss the best qualities of a friend. List a few of those qualities here.

_____

_____

_____

_____

Compare your list to the qualities listed below:

- Honesty
- Loyalty
- Good judgment
- Kindness

What great qualities to find in friends, not to mention in ourselves! Try to define these traits, and during the week, look for these qualities in yourself and others.

Share your ideas and discuss three things you can do to avoid dangerous company. List them here.

1. _____
2. _____
3. _____

You've heard it said that birds of a feather flock together.

Actually, birds that flock together *become* birds of the same feather.

Think about it!

Action Ideas

Pick out a nice card and make some cookies to take to one of your friends. Or take your friend a "just because" balloon!

Words to Memorize

Do not follow the crowd in doing wrong.
Exodus 23:2

Your Goal for This Week

_____

_____

_____

Closing Prayer

Lord, help me to choose friends who will encourage me to do good.

Week Four

ARE YOU FOR WHAT'S RIGHT?

Scripture Reading for This Week

Romans 8:37–39

No, in all these things we are more than conquerors through him who loved us. For I am convinced that neither death nor life, neither angels nor demons, neither the present nor the future, nor any powers, neither height nor depth, nor anything else in all creation, will be able to separate us from the love of God that is in Christ Jesus our Lord.

What words best describe the main point of this passage? Write them in the space below.

*Daughter*_____

Mom _____

Tell each other why you chose these words.

$\mathcal{M}$y daughter Jennifer took a psychology course during her senior year in a public high school. Her teacher gave an assignment for each of the students to choose a controversial topic and take a position for or against it. Each student needed to research the topic, write a paper about it, and then present to the class the position he or she had taken.

Jennifer decided on the topic of abortion, knowing it to be a very controversial issue. She chose to stand *against* abortion. From teaching at home, her own study of the Bible, and teaching by different Sunday school teachers and youth leaders, she remembered that Psalm 139 says "we are fearfully and wonderfully made."

Jennifer thoroughly researched her paper before presenting it to her class. She wasn't surprised, but she was disappointed to see that most of her classmates disagreed with her thinking. Over and over people told her that abortion was a choice each woman should be able to make for herself. Most of her class thought she was out of touch with what is happening in the real world today.

Her teacher was a Christian, and he agreed with Jennifer's position, but because of school policy he could not openly speak for her. So she basically stood alone.

How do you think Jennifer felt at this point? How would you feel at this point?

Jennifer was discouraged because her classmates were so strongly for abortion. She wondered whether or not they understood what is really involved with abortion. She wondered if there was something she could have said that would have changed their minds or if they were just determined to believe what they already believed.

She was sad that so many people her age were misinformed and misguided concerning abortion. She hoped that her classmates would at least think about what she had said.

Jennifer felt alone in her convictions. At the same time she was thankful for her knowledge of the Scriptures and the encouragement to stand firm in her convictions.

What the Story Says

It's always better to do the right thing, but sometimes doing the right thing requires a lot of courage.

Discussion Questions

1. How would you have handled the topic if you had been in Jennifer's place?
2. How might she have responded if she had not relied on God to give her courage?
3. How would Jennifer have felt if she'd decided to change her position because of the pressure of her classmates?

DEFINITION OF RIGHT:
    What is just, good, and proper.

DEFINITION OF COURAGE:
    Mental or moral strength to withstand danger, fear, or difficulty.

What Does the Bible Say?

Look up the following Scriptures and fill in the blanks.

Isaiah 40:29
He gives _____ to the weary and _____
the power of the weak.

How does God give us strength when we need it?

Psalm 31:24
Be strong and take heart, all you who _____ in the Lord.

What does it mean to take heart?

Psalm 23:4
Even though I walk through the valley of the shadow of death, I will _____, for you are with me; your rod and your staff, they comfort me.

John 14:27
Peace I leave with you; my peace I give you. I do not give to you as the world gives. Do not let your hearts be _____ and do not be _____.

Looking Deeper

For Mom:

Tell your daughter about a time when it was difficult for you to stand up for what was right. Summarize it below.

_____

_____

_____

_____

_____

_____

For Daughter:

Tell your mother about a time that it was hard for you to do the right thing. Write it below.

_____

_____

_____

_____

In what ways may you be asked to stand up for your convictions in the next five years? List them below. Your mother should also list answers.

_____

_____

_____

_____

_____

_____

_____

Compare your list to these possibilities:

1. Like Jennifer, you may be forced to defend your faith in Christ.
2. You may have a chance to befriend someone who has chosen to have her baby or give her baby up for adoption. Will you show her God's love and take time with her?
3. You may find that all your friends disagree with something you believe. Will you be strong enough to stand

alone in your convictions to follow what God's Word says is right and avoid what is wrong?

4. You may need to find the courage to tell the truth when you know the truth will cause you problems.

※ ※ ※

A seventh-grade boy in Arkansas carried his Bible to school every day. Three boys approached him, grabbed the Bible, and said, "You sissy. Religion is for sissies. Prayer is for sissies. Don't ever bring this Bible back to school again."

He handed the Bible back to the biggest one of the three and said, "Here, see if you've got enough courage to carry this around school just one day."

He made three friends.

For Mom:

Discuss with your daughter and then list below some of the tips that helped you find the courage to stand up for what's right when it was difficult.

_____

_____

_____

_____

_____

_____

_____

_____

Identify and discuss three God-given qualities your daughter possesses that will help her face these challenges. Write them below.

1. _____

2. _____

3. _____

How can she use these qualities on a daily basis?

_____

_____

_____

Super! Now you have a plan. Try practicing it this week.

Action Ideas

Read Psalm 139 and discuss it. Set up an appointment together at the local crisis pregnancy center to see the ministry it is having in your city. Maybe you could ask the coordinator if there are ways for you to help out.

Words to Memorize

Be strong and take heart, all you who hope in the Lord.
Psalm 31:24

Your Goal for This Week

_____

_____

_____

Closing Prayer

Lord, help me to always have the courage to stand up for what's right.

Section Two

HAPPILY EVER AFTER...

Week Five

THE GROWING STRUGGLE

Scripture Reading for This Week

Isaiah 43:1–3
But now, this is what the Lord says—he who created you, O Jacob, he who formed you, O Israel: "Fear not, for I have redeemed you; I have summoned you by name; you are mine. When you pass through the waters, I will be with you; and when you pass through the rivers, they will not sweep over you. When you walk through the fire, you will not be burned; the flames will not set you ablaze. For I am the Lord, your God, the Holy One of Israel, your Savior."

What words best describe the main point of these verses? Write them in the space below.

Daughter _____

Mom _____

Tell each other why you chose these words.

*C*ortney woke at the rooster's crowing. Her eyes popped open, blinked at the ceiling for a moment, then closed again as she snuggled deeper into the feather mattress and inhaled the crisp scent of sheets dried in country sunshine.

Granny's house.

Cortney loved her summer visits to Granny's farm. As she lazily rolled out of bed, the sights and sounds of the Illinois prairie composed a peaceful symphony for the senses.

On the farm there was no homework to do and no classes to attend, except for the lessons she learned helping Grandpa care for the farm animals. But each day, Cortney looked forward to those lessons. She had left the noisy streets and pollution behind in Los Angeles, along with two pesky brothers who constantly teased her and generally drove her crazy. There would be none of that at Granny's house. Just long, hardworking but enjoyable days exploring the wonders of nature and evenings cuddled with Granny on the sofa as she read aloud from Dickens, Lewis, and Lawhead.

And this summer promised to be better than ever. *After all, I'm twelve now,* Cortney thought to herself while dressing. *Grandpa promised to let me break a colt when I was twelve. I can hardly wait.*

After she dressed, Cortney ran downstairs to find Granny. She spotted her through the kitchen window on the sprawling veranda of the old farmhouse.

"Good morning," Cortney said as she pushed open the screen door and walked out onto the porch.

"Did you sleep well, Cortney?" Granny's eyes twinkled at the sight of her only granddaughter.

"Like a brand new kitten," Cortney purred, squinting at the daylight. She yawned deeply, drinking in the pungent smell of hay and alfalfa mingled with the fragrance of the lilacs bordering the porch.

Granny stood at the edge of the porch rail. "Come look at

this." She waved for Cortney to come closer, then looked up, craning her neck to stare at something in the eaves.

"What is it?" Cortney asked as she stepped to Granny's side.

"It's a cocoon. I've watched it for a couple of weeks now." Granny pointed a weathered finger at a crinkled cocoon dangling from a wood beam. "In just a few days a butterfly will emerge."

"A butterfly?" Cortney stretched to her full height on the tips of her toes to get a better look.

"Yes, the cocoon will split open, and little by little the butterfly will begin to break free. Oh, by the way, Cortney . . ." Granny cupped Cortney's chin in the palm of her hand, "when this happens, don't try to help it. Let the butterfly free itself. Do you promise?"

"OK," Cortney agreed.

During the next few days, Cortney checked the cocoon for changes once every morning, and then again in the afternoon. Finally, late in the afternoon of the fourth day, she noticed that the cocoon appeared to be vibrating. It moved this way and then that, shivering. Pulling a patio chair closer, she stood on top of the chair to watch. Cortney wished she could run and get her grandmother so she could watch too, but she had gone to the store.

Within a few minutes, the cocoon split open and Cortney could see a wet butterfly folded tightly inside, beating its wings wildly against the cocoon to get out. But it seemed unable to free itself. As Cortney watched the frantic labor of the helpless creature, a pang of compassion welled up within her. She wanted so much to help, but she remembered her promise to Granny. So she just waited and watched.

Thirty minutes passed, but still the cocoon held the butterfly captive. Finally, the butterfly became so passionate in its attempt to get out of its prison that Cortney could resist no longer. On an impulse, she climbed from her chair to the top of the banister.

Clinging to a post with one arm to steady herself, she reached as far as she could, pushed a thumb and index finger into the opening of the cocoon, and split open the two halves.

The butterfly sprang free. For just a moment it fluttered in midair in an attempt to spread its wings, but, failing, it dropped to the porch floor. It flopped around briefly like a tiny beached fish, then suddenly it became very still.

"Oh, no!" Cortney gasped in disbelief. Jumping down from her perch, she picked up the pitiful creature and set it in the palm of her hand. She nudged it gently with her finger, then watched for movement. But it didn't move. It was dead.

"Granny!" Cortney moaned.

Within minutes Granny was back home. "What is it, Cortney?" she asked, the sorrow on her granddaughter's face revealing her distress. "What's wrong?"

"Oh, Granny," Cortney mourned, her sad eyes filling with tears that began to spill over onto her cheeks, "it's dead! The butterfly is dead!"

When Granny saw what had happened, she sat down in a nearby rocker. Cortney sat on the chair beside her with her head in her hands.

"Cortney, did you open the cocoon?" Granny asked.

Cortney nodded. "I just wanted to help."

"I know. You just didn't understand." Granny patted her arm. "You see, the butterfly must be fit to survive outside the cocoon. It struggles against the cocoon to strengthen its muscles enough to fly."

"I'm sorry," Cortney whispered, laying her head on Granny's soft shoulder.

"That's OK, Cortney," Granny hugged her tightly. "You know, the cocoon kinda reminds me of you."

"Huh?" Cortney sat upright, looking straight into Granny's eyes.

"Well, when you were small, you were like the fuzzy caterpillar—not yet what you would become. Now, you're in-between—

like the cocoon. You're old enough to do a lot of new things at home and on the farm, but you're not yet an adult. As you grow in the next few years, life will present you with struggles and challenges. When you deal with these challenges, you'll sometimes feel like the butterfly beating hard against its cocoon."

"You mean like the challenges of bratty brothers?" Cortney grinned.

"Yes," Granny threw her head back and laughed heartily. "But you'll have a lot of other problems too." She tweaked Cortney's nose. "Just remember when things get tough, you may be tempted to find an easy way out, but it's the struggle that will make you strong and prepare you for your role as a woman."

Granny paused, then added, "Do you understand what I mean?"

"I think so," Cortney said. "You mean that I shouldn't always try to avoid hard things. Sometimes hard things are even good, like for the butterfly."

Granny nodded and smiled. Cortney laid her head back on Granny's shoulder and watched the colt she would start breaking tomorrow trotting ahead of its mother and her grandfather. Cortney and Granny rocked lazily back and forth on the old farmhouse porch as the sunset settled over the Illinois prairie, painting the sky crimson and blue.

What the Story Says

Growing up demands a struggle,
and there is no easy way out.

Discussion Questions

1. What are some of the struggles you face each day?

2. Do you think these struggles will increase as you grow older?

3. Do you sometimes feel like the tightly folded butterfly trapped inside the cocoon? If so, how does that feel?

DEFINITION OF STRUGGLE:
> To make strenuous or violent efforts against opposition; to proceed with great difficulty.

What Does the Bible Say?

Look up the following Scriptures and fill in the blanks.

Colossians 1:10
And we pray this in order that you may live a life _____ of the Lord and may _____ him in every way: bearing fruit in every good work, growing in the _____ of God.

Colossians 1:11
Being strengthened with all _____ according to his glorious _____ so that you may have great endurance and patience.

2 Peter 3:18
But grow in the _____ and _____ of our Lord and Savior Jesus Christ. To him be glory both now and forever! Amen.

What are some ways you can grow?

Ephesians 3:20
Now to him who is able to do immeasurably _____
than all we ask or imagine, according to his _____
that is at work within us.

1 Peter 1:7
These have come so that your _____—of greater
worth than gold, which perishes even though refined by fire—
may be proved _____ and may result in
praise, glory and honor when Jesus Christ is revealed.

What does it mean to be genuine?

Word Scramble

1. wrepo _____

2. aergc _____

3. enwokelgd _____

(For answers to this and other word scrambles, see page
196.)

Looking Deeper

For Mom:

Tell your daughter about the biggest challenges you faced when
you were her age. Discuss them with her and then list them below.

_____

_____

_____

List and discuss the three biggest struggles you think your daughter will face in the next five years.

1. _____

2. _____

3. _____

For Discussion:

Together, compare your list to these possibilities:

- Boys!
- Friendships
- Relationships at home
- Peer pressure
- Demands at school
- Keeping herself pure

For Daughter:

What do you think you can do that will help you deal with these challenges?

_____

_____

_____

For Mom:

Tell your daughter the tips that have been most helpful to you. Write them down here.

_____

_____

_____

_____

Discuss and identify three God-given qualities your daughter possesses that will help her face these challenges. Write them below.

1. _____

2. _____

3. _____

For Daughter:

How can you use these qualities on a daily basis to help you grow? If you have trouble thinking of ways, your mother may have some suggestions.

_____

_____

_____

Action Ideas

WHO I WAS . . .   WHO I AM . . .
(find a photo)   (find a photo)

WHO I'D LIKE TO BE!
Take time and think about this.
Write down (or draw) some of your
goals and dreams.

Words to Memorize

But grow in the grace and knowledge
of our Lord and Savior Jesus Christ.
2 Peter 3:18

Your Goal for This Week

_____

_____

_____

Closing Prayer

Lord, help me in my struggles to grow as a woman of God.

Week Six

FOREVER FRIENDS

Scripture Reading for This Week

Ecclesiastes 4:9–12

Two are better than one, because they have a good return for their work: If one falls down, his friend can help him up. But pity the man who falls and has no one to help him up! Also, if two lie down together, they will keep warm. But how can one keep warm alone? Though one may be overpowered, two can defend themselves. A cord of three strands is not quickly broken.

What words best describe the main point of these verses? Write them in the space below.

Daughter_____

Mom _____

Tell each other why you chose these words.

*D*o you have a friend you love enough to die for?

This is the story of such a friendship. Two young men, Damon and Pythias, lived in the small town of Syracuse, nestled against the scorched hillsides of Sicily. They had grown up in the same neighborhood, playing games and roaming the familiar streets together. As they grew into young men, their friendship continued and matured into a deep brotherly love. Damon and Pythias were the best of friends.

In those days, a tyrant named Dionysius ruled Syracuse. He had earned his reputation as a cruel oppressor by executing people on whims when anything happened to displease or anger him. The whole community lived in constant fear of his next violent outburst.

Damon was very angry about the injustices he had seen and the fact that this cruel tyrant continued to get away with them. His rage at the dictator's atrocities had become a topic of debate between him and his friend. "I have to do something about these injustices," Damon told Pythias. "I can't just stand by and do nothing!"

But Pythias always tried to reason with him. "You'll risk your life if you do anything!" he told Damon, concerned for his friend's safety. "And besides," Pythias reminded him, "what can one man do?" Pythias knew his friend well. He knew the passion that simmered just beneath the surface and boiled over at times like this when Damon found a cause for his passion.

Pythias was right, though, and Damon knew it. One person could not make a difference if he acted by himself. So Damon began to consider how he could bring the community together in a revolt to overthrow Dionysius. Damon canvassed his neighborhood and invited neighbors and friends to meet at his house one evening to discuss what could be done.

Secretly Damon doubted that more than a handful of those he spoke with would summon the courage to participate in his forum. Everyone was so afraid.

That night six neighbors made their way in the darkness to Damon's home. They huddled together around the dining table and discussed in hushed voices what might be done.

"We have to do something!" Damon told them. "We can't just allow this brute to continue terrorizing us." His dark eyes sparked with youthful intensity. They dismissed an hour later without any real answers to their dilemma. But they agreed to meet again the following evening to continue their discussion.

Word of their meetings quickly spread through the town. Before long, the rumors reached the tyrant's ears.

Dionysius immediately dispatched spies to watch and identify the leader of this rebellion. Within two days, the spies reported their findings, and Dionysius ordered his soldiers to arrest Damon and bring him to his court chambers.

The soldiers arrested Damon and brought him to Dionysius, who ordered the soldiers to execute him the next day. But Damon begged Dionysius to first allow him to go home to say farewell to his parents and family.

The tyrant couldn't believe his ears. "Why should I set you free?" He scowled at Damon. "You will surely run away to escape your punishment."

"I give my word!" Damon pleaded.

"Your word!" scoffed the tyrant.

"I will take his place," a voice called from the crowd. The mass of onlookers scuffled out of the way as Pythias pushed his way through the crowd to the front and stepped toward Dionysius. He summoned his courage. "I will take Damon's place until he returns. And if he does not return . . ." Pythias said, swallowing hard, "put me to death instead."

Stunned by this sudden and profound expression of love and trust, Dionysius momentarily lost the edge on his anger as he sat dumbfounded, his mouth hanging open. He regathered his senses quickly, though, as he pointed a bony finger in Damon's face. "I will give you exactly six hours. Not one minute longer. And if you do not return, your friend will die in your place. Don't underestimate me!" he roared. "I won't hesitate!"

And with that, the ruler turned to face Pythias. "You are an utter fool!" he declared, then snapped his fingers in the direction of the guards, who immediately seized Pythias and took him into custody.

"I will return, my friend," Damon called over his shoulder as he ran from the chamber.

Five hours passed. Huddled on moldy straw in the corner of a dark cell, Pythias shifted from one hip to the other. He cocked his head toward the bolted door as the echo of footsteps grew louder in the hallway outside his cell. The footsteps stopped outside his door. "Five hours now," a guard jeered. "Your so-called friend has abandoned you. He laughs at your foolishness right now." The guard snorted as his footfalls faded away.

Another forty-five minutes passed and Damon had not returned—fifteen minutes left before his deadline! The guards brought Pythias from the cell and presented him to the ruler for execution.

"It looks like your friend has left you to die," Dionysius said as he smirked at Pythias.

"Damon is my true friend," Pythias answered. "He has become ill or been hurt or else he would be here."

"Call for the executioner," the ruler ordered.

Pythias prepared himself to die, still confident in Damon's loyalty.

The guards grabbed Pythias and ushered him to the executioner. The next thing Pythias knew his head was shoved down on the beheading block, and the executioner's sword was raised, ready to come crashing down on his neck. Suddenly, Damon rushed through the chamber doors, yelling "Stop! Stop! I am here!"

Damon ran to embrace his friend, out of breath. "My horse died and I had trouble finding another," Damon explained. The two friends continued to embrace each other.

Pythias suddenly broke free of his friend's arms and turned to Dionysius. "Let me die for my friend," he pleaded.

The tyrant stared in wonder at the scene he was witnessing. "What!" he said, astounded. "You are willing to die in your friend's place? Are you serious?" he demanded.

Damon argued, "No! I will bear my own punishment!"

The cruel ruler's cold old heart was touched for the first time in many years. It began to thaw. Legend has it that Dionysius was so moved by this demonstration of true affection that he released both of the friends with one request: that he be allowed to find out from them what made their friendship so strong—even in the face of death.

What the Story Says
True friendship makes sacrifices.

Discussion Questions

1. Why do you think Pythias was willing to die for his friend?

2. If the roles had been reversed and it was Pythias who was sentenced to die, do you think Damon would have offered his life for his friend? Why or why not?

3. Do you have a friend or a relative you love enough to die for? When is it a good thing to be loyal to friends? When is it a bad thing?

DEFINITION OF FRIEND:
   A person who knows, loves, and trusts another person.

What Does the Bible Say?

Look up the following Scriptures and fill in the blanks.

John 15:13
Greater_____ has no one than this, that he lay down his
_____ for his friends.

Romans 12:10
Be _____ to one another in brotherly love.
Honor one another _____ yourselves.

1 Peter 1:22
Now that you have purified yourselves by obeying the truth so
that you have sincere _____ for your brothers, _____
one another deeply, from the heart.

Proverbs 18:24
There is a _____ who sticks closer than a brother.

*Human friendships are great, but there is an even better friend-
ship—we can be friends of God. Abraham was called "the Friend
of God" (James 2:23 KJV). He loved and trusted in God, and God
loved and trusted him, too.*

John 15:14
You are my _____ if you do what I command.

Who said that?

_____

Puzzle

Make an acrostic with the word friend. What are some words
that describe friendship for you?

F
R
I
E
N
D

Looking Deeper

For Discussion:

God's Word tells us to be encouragers of one another. Each of you write down the names of three people you are going to encourage this week. Be creative in your ways of encouragement. It could end up being a lot of fun!

Daughter: *Mom:*

_____   _____

_____   _____

_____   _____

For Mom:

Tell your daughter about one of your close friendships. How does this friend enrich your life?

_____

_____

_____

For Daughter:

Tell your mother about your closest friend. What kind of things do you like most about her (or him)?

_____

_____

_____

🏵 🏵 🏵

Just after the Civil War, the caretaker of a cemetery watched a man place flowers on a grave every week. Finally, he asked the man, "You must love the person who is buried there very much. Was he your father?"

"No," the man replied.

"Was he your brother?"

"No," he answered again.

"Then he must have been your son?" The caretaker was sure he had guessed correctly this time.

"No," the man replied. "He was my dearest friend."

"You must have loved him very much."

"I owe him my life," the man told the caretaker. "When I was drafted to go to war, he took my place so that I might stay at home to care for my wife and children. He was killed in battle. He died for me."

List three qualities you look for in a great friendship.

1. _____

2. _____

3. _____

Compare your list to these possibilities:

- A person who is loyal
- Someone who is kind and considerate
- Someone you can trust to keep secrets
- Someone who will be on your side
- An honest person
- Someone who knows how to have fun
- A person who will do the right thing even when it's hard

For Mom:

Tell your daughter the ways you have learned to be a better friend.

_____

_____

_____

_____

For Discussion:

How can we be friends with God? Discuss and then list a few of your ideas below.

_____

_____

_____

_____

Compare your ideas with those below:

- Talk to God throughout your day. Tell Him your joys, struggles, and disappointments.
- Read your Bible every day to discover more about God.
- Do something each day to show God your love for Him.

Now you have a plan. Try practicing it this week.

Words to Memorize
A friend loves at all times.
Proverbs 17:17

Your Goal for This Week

Closing Prayer

Dear Lord, help me to love and care for my friends as You love and care for me.

Week Seven

BE ALL YOU CAN BE

Scripture Reading for This Week

Jeremiah 29:10–14

"I will come to you and fulfill my gracious promise to bring you back to this place. For I know the plans I have for you," declares the Lord, "plans to prosper you and not to harm you, plans to give you hope and a future. Then you will call upon me and come and pray to me, and I will listen to you. You will seek me and find me when you seek me with all your heart. I will be found by you," declares the Lord.

What words best describe the main point of these verses? Write them in the space below.

Daughter _____

Mom _____

Tell each other why you chose these words.

It was September 17, 1994. In the Atlantic City Convention Center, the Seventy-fifth Annual Miss America Pageant was in its final night of competition. Before the evening ended, a new Miss America would be crowned.

The five finalists had been selected. Anticipation hung heavily in the convention hall as families, friends, and supporters of the pageant participants waited anxiously for the announcement naming Miss America 1995.

The five finalists stood smiling on stage with host Regis Philbin. They all looked elegant in their evening gowns, and each one maintained a poised stage presence in spite of the obvious excitement.

One of the finalists was Miss Alabama, Heather Whitestone. Heather had been deaf since she was eighteen months old, when she fought for her life against a serious illness that left her in a world of silence. During the talent phase of the pageant competition, she had proven her slogan, "Anything Is Possible!" For her performance, she danced to Sandi Patty's "Via Dolorosa"—music she could not hear—and drew repeated ovations from a spellbound audience.

For Heather, the dream to win the title of "Miss America" did not begin four years earlier when she competed in her first local pageant. The seeds of that dream were planted almost twenty years earlier in an Alabama hospital.

While she was growing up, things most people took for granted every day were challenges for Heather. During her elementary school years, she had huge problems communicating. For years Heather worked until late every night to overcome these disadvantages. She believes that even then God had a plan for her.

Actually, Heather fooled even her doctors, who had predicted she would never go beyond third grade in her studies. She showed them! She got As and Bs in college.

All her life Heather had challenged the limitations of her disability.

Who would have guessed a little deaf girl could become a ballerina? But Heather was determined in her ballet disciplines. For years she practiced, sometimes several hours a day, with a teacher who could hear the music. During these lessons, Heather taught herself to feel the vibrations of the music with her feet and body. Then she memorized the music and counted her way through a choreographed number.

Now, on national television, Heather had danced across a stage in Atlantic City and into the hearts of millions of Americans.

※ ※ ※

Finally, the moment everyone had waited for arrived. The scores had been tallied, and during the commercial break, one of the judges handed Regis an envelope with the results.

Heather held tightly to her dream as she and four other young women faced their destinies with their hands clasped together.

Regis opened the envelope and held the card in front of him as he read, "Fourth runner-up . . . Miss Indiana, Tiffany Storm." The audience applauded and cheered. Once the noise died down, he continued, "Third runner-up . . . Miss Georgia, Andrea Krahn." More applause and cheers.

Three contestants remained at center stage holding hands.

"Second runner-up . . ." Regis read again from the card, "Miss New Jersey, Jennifer Alexis Makris."

After the applause died down, a hush fell over the audience as they awaited the moment they had all come for.

"Here we are now. Down to two. That leaves Miss Alabama and Miss Virginia. OK. This is it, everybody! Ladies and gentlemen, the first runner-up is . . . Miss Virginia, Cullen Johnson. And the new Miss America 1995, Miss Alabama, Heather Whitestone!"

Thirteen thousand people rose to their feet in a standing ovation.

Meanwhile, Heather hadn't been able to read Regis's lips as

he announced the winner. She didn't realize what had just happened. Then the runner-up, Cullen Johnson, turned to face Heather. She pointed her finger at her and mouthed, "It's you!"

For the first time in the competition's seventy-five-year history, a woman with a disability was crowned Miss America.

As Miss America, Heather spoke to thousands of young people across the United States, encouraging them to be all they can be. She told them, "If you can dream a dream, you too can accomplish it according to God's will." Of course, that does not mean that every wish a person has will be fulfilled. But God gives each person talents, skills, and interests, and He uses those to show people what they can do for Him.

Heather told her audiences, "He promises that 'he who began a good work in you will carry it on to completion until the day of Christ Jesus.' I pray that you will recognize the need for God's help and believe in miracles from Him. Hold fast to God's words and His strength through Jesus, and watch your dreams come true."

If God wants you to do something—even something that looks impossible—He will give you everything you need to do it.

What the Story Says
Set your sights on Christ,
for in Him there are no limitations.

Discussion Questions

1. Put your fingers in your ears and try to imagine what it would be like to never hear anything. How do you think that would feel?

2. What are some of the difficulties Heather had to over-come because of her deafness?

3. Where did she find the strength to keep trying in spite of her limitations?

What Does the Bible Say?

Look up the following Scriptures and fill in the blanks.

Philippians 1:6
He who began a _____ in you will carry it on
to _____ until the day of Christ Jesus.

Matthew 19:26
Jesus looked at them and said, With man this is _____,
but with God all things are_____.

Philippians 4:8
Finally, brothers, whatever is_____, whatever
is_____, whatever is _____, whatever is
_____, whatever is _____, whatever is
_____—if anything is excellent or praiseworthy—
think about such things.

2 Timothy 2:15
Do your best to present yourself to God as one_____, a
workman who does not need to be _____ and who
correctly handles the word of truth.

Matthew 6:33
But seek _____ his kingdom and his _____, and
all these things will be given to you as well.

Ephesians 3:20
Now to him who is able to do immeasurably more than all we
_____ or _____, according to his
power that is at work within us, to him be glory in the church.

Looking Deeper

Anything Within God's Will Is Possible.

Heather developed a five-point STARS program that she discussed at the Miss America competition:

> **S** uccess
> **T** hrough
> **A** ction and
> **R** ealization of your
> dream **S**

For Daughter:

What are some ways you can start planning for your future?

1. You can have a positive attitude when you have to do something you don't want to do (including homework, chores, and being nice to somebody you don't really like). Hard work helps develop us to be what God wants us to be.

2. You can realize that God made you able to dream big dreams. Maybe not all of them will come true, but if you work hard and if He wants them to, they will.

3. Even becoming Miss America is not like having a wish fulfilled with a magic wand. Understand that all plans take a lot of work.

4. Be smart enough to know when your dreams don't

match what you're good at doing.

5. Thank God that He has given you your family to encourage you and help you meet your goals. And thank Him for your loyal friends too.

For Mom:

Tell your daughter of your dreams when you were her age. List them below.

_____

_____

_____

_____

For Daughter:

Tell your mom about your dreams for the future. List them briefly below.

_____

_____

_____

_____

Discuss and list some of the challenges you might face while trying to make your dreams come true.

_____

_____

_____

_____

Discuss and identify three God-given talents your daughter possesses that might help her fulfill her goals for the future. Write them below.

1. _____

2. _____

3. _____

How can she develop these talents on a daily basis?

_____

_____

_____

For Daughter:

Compare your mother's ideas with the possibilities below:

- Offer your talents back to God for His use.
- If you are gifted musically, look for ways to be the best musician you can be and glorify God with your music.
- If you have the gift of encouragement, look for creative ways to encourage others daily.

Cool! Now you have a plan. Try practicing it this week.

Action Ideas

Do a service project: rake leaves, wash someone's car, help an elderly person clean his or her house, walk your neighbor's dog. You could also make a "coupon book" with services you will provide for one of your neighbors or an older couple in your church.

Words to Memorize

He who began a good work in you
will carry it on to completion.
Philippians 1:6

Your Goal for This Week

_____

_____

_____

Closing Prayer

Lord, help me to be the best that I can be and glorify You in all I do.

Week Eight

LOVE FOREVER AND A DAY

Scripture Reading for This Week

Proverbs 31:10–31

A wife of noble character who can find? She is worth far more than rubies. Her husband has full confidence in her and lacks nothing of value.

She brings him good, not harm, all the days of her life. She selects wool and flax and works with eager hands. She is like the merchant ships, bringing her food from afar. She gets up while it is still dark; she provides food for her family and portions for her servant girls.

She considers a field and buys it; out of her earnings she plants a vineyard. She sets about her work vigorously; her arms are strong for her tasks. She sees that her trading is profitable, and her lamp does not go out at night.

In her hand she holds the distaff and grasps the spindle with her fingers. She opens her arms to the poor and extends her hands to the needy.

When it snows, she has no fear for her household; for all of them are clothed in scarlet. She makes coverings for her bed; she is clothed in fine linen and purple.

Her husband is respected at the city gate, where he takes his seat among the elders of the land. She makes linen garments and sells them, and supplies the merchants with sashes.

She is clothed with strength and dignity; she can laugh at the days to come. She speaks with wisdom, and faithful instruction is on her tongue.

She watches over the affairs of her household and does not eat the bread of idleness. Her children arise and call her blessed; her husband also, and he praises her: "Many women do noble things, but you surpass them all."

Charm is deceptive, and beauty is fleeting; but a woman who fears the Lord is to be praised. Give her the reward she has earned, and let her works bring her praise at the city gate.

*H*owever you feel about boys right now, there will probably come a day when you will want to fall in love with someone and look for many of your dreams to be fulfilled in marriage and a family. When that day comes, what qualities will you look for in a lifetime mate?

Will he be tall, dark, and handsome? Or stocky, rugged, and outdoorsy?

Will he charm and entertain you with his wit? Or will he be the strong, silent type?

What kind of person would be compatible with your personality? What kind of qualities would be needed to create a happy family life? Even more important, what qualities will *you* need to become a godly wife and mother?

These are some of the questions you'll want to ask yourself when you begin your search for Mr. Right.

Jillian had asked these questions and many others. At twenty-one years old she was marrying Mark at Neighborhood Church in Ventura, California. In less than an hour, she would change her name to his.

She stood straight and tall in her sparkling white gown at the back of the sanctuary beside her proud father. Her dark hair formed a flounce of curls that nestled against her neck, striking a contrast against the pristine white of her veil.

The sanctuary was a sea of white. Pots of lilies had been lined up two feet deep along the platform. A white runner covered the center aisle, leading down to the front. At the far end of that aisle stood Mark in a white tuxedo, looking more handsome than she'd ever seen him. His eyes rested on hers; his smile beckoned her to start her walk toward him as the organ swelled in the prelude of "The Bridal March."

Jillian had first met Mark at church. They had dated through most of high school and were in youth group together. In Jillian's senior year they began discussing marriage, but they decided to wait to get married until Mark finished college and Jillian was well on her way to finishing. Now she had one more year to complete her degree in physical education.

Six months before the wedding they began planning the ceremony. While they prepared for their wedding, at the same time they prepared for their marriage by taking premarital counseling with their pastor. He had assigned them to read numerous books on marriage, which they did. They felt as prepared as they could be to deal with the challenges of the first few years of married life.

Both families knew each other well and had given their blessings. But most important, both Jillian and Mark had committed their lives to Christ and planned their marriage to be a team ministry under His leadership. They had this very important aspect in common, and they had committed their future together to Christ.

And now here they were, repeating their vows before Pastor Bennett. They finished with, "to love, honor, and cherish until death do us part."

"I do," they both promised, with rings to seal that promise.

And finally the pastor said, "Mark, you may kiss the bride."

With that, Mark scooped Jillian into his arms and placed a kiss on her lips that she would remember forever.

Everyone beamed and then broke into applause as the new couple made their way up the aisle and into their future together.

❧ ❧ ❧

Meanwhile, across town in the County Courthouse Building, another wedding was taking place.

Rachel and Garrett had scheduled an appointment to be married in the judge's chambers. Their best friends, Sharon and Jonathan, joined them for this celebration.

Rachel looked sweet in her pink satin dress. She was eighteen and had just finished high school in June. As yet she had no plans for college. "I don't know what I want to do," she told her friends. "I've got lots of time to figure that out." First, she wanted to have a little fun before she settled down with a family of her own.

Garrett had graduated from high school a year ago and went to work for a local tire company. He made enough money to take care of his car, rent a tiny apartment on the Avenue, and put a little food on the table. He figured that when Rachel got a job, they would have enough money to pay their bills and have some fun at the same time.

Rachel and Garrett had met in school and dated for almost two years. They made a handsome couple with Rachel's cheerleader looks and Garrett's athletic build. In fact, Rachel thought Garrett was the cutest guy in all of Ventura County, and he made life seem like one long roller-coaster ride. She loved the exhilaration of being with him.

Rachel had spent some time at Garrett's house, but she tried to stay away from his parents. Even though they didn't go to church and didn't call themselves Christians like her family did, they were very conservative. Like Rachel's parents, they thought

Rachel and Garrett were too young to get married and they wanted them to wait a year or two.

Garrett and Rachel had decided to go ahead and get married anyway. They figured they were old enough to know what they wanted out of life—and it wasn't the traditional path their parents had taken. In fact, their first goal, as soon as they could put a little money together, was to tour Europe together.

Now they stood before the judge, happily taking their vows "to love, honor, and cherish until death do us part." They would show everyone that their way would work as well as the traditional approach.

And so two couples entered the future with great hopes and dreams, each with visions of what that future would be.

What the Story Says

Something as important as the choice of a lifetime mate deserves the most careful consideration.

Discussion Questions

1. Do you think the characteristics that will make a good husband are different from the ones that make a great date?

2. Does Rachel and Garrett's marriage have the same chance for success as Jillian and Mark's? Why or why not?

3. What are some of the strengths the first couple brought to their marriage?

What Does the Bible Say?

Look up the following Scriptures and fill in the blanks.

2 Corinthians 6:14
Do not be _____ together with _____.
For what do righteousness and wickedness have in common? Or
what fellowship can light have with darkness?

What does it mean to be "yoked together"?

Regarding the qualities of a husband:
Ephesians 5:25, 28–30
Husbands, _____ your wives, just as Christ loved the church
and gave himself up for her. . . . In this same way, husbands
ought to _____ their wives as their own bodies. He who
loves his wife loves himself. After all, no one ever _____ his
own body, but he feeds and cares for it, just as Christ does the
church—for we are members of his body.

1 Timothy 6:11
But you, man of God, flee from all this, and pursue righteousness, godliness, faith, love, endurance and gentleness.

*List the characteristics in this verse that God expects men to
pursue.*

R _____
G _____
F _____
L _____
E _____
G _____

1 Peter 3:7
Husbands, in the same way be _____ as you live
with your wives, and treat them with _____ as
the weaker partner and as heirs with you of the gracious gift of
life, so that nothing will hinder your prayers.

What does it mean to be considerate?
How can someone show you respect?

Regarding the qualities of a wife:
Proverbs 12:4
A wife of noble character is her husband's _____, but
a disgraceful wife is like _____ in his bones.

Which would you rather be compared to?

Ephesians 5:33
However, each one of you also must love his wife as he loves himself, and the wife must respect her husband.

How might you show respect for someone?

Looking Deeper

For Discussion:

What are some of the qualities the Bible says make a desirable
wife? Discuss and then list them below. (Don't forget to look at
Proverbs 31.)

_____

_____

_____

_____

Compare your list to the following possibilities:

- Trustworthy
- Creative
- Hardworking
- Takes care of her health
- Uses financial common sense
- Good steward of her money
- Compassionate
- A good parent
- A believer
- Optimistic
- Pure

Which of these qualities would also make a desirable husband?

_____

_____

_____

For Daughter:

Discuss and agree on some things you can do in the next five years to prepare for your future marriage. List them below.

_____

_____

_____

_____

Did your list include prayer? It's never too soon to start praying for the man who will become your husband. Prayers have an impact across the miles on that special person.

List some things you might pray about.

_____

_____

_____

_____

_____

_____

Compare your list to these possibilities:

- Pray for the salvation of your future husband.
- Pray for the qualities in him that you listed above to grow.
- Pray for God's blessing and protection on him.
- Pray that God will show him His perfect will for his life.
- Pray that he will keep himself pure.

Which of these prayers do you need to pray for yourself as well?

_____

_____

_____

What are some of the advantages of praying for your future?

_____

_____

_____

Compare your list to the following possibilities:

- Through the dating years, your prayers will remind you that you belong to God.
- Your prayers will remind you that your future spouse belongs to God.
- Your prayers will give you direction for the future, allowing you to trust your life to God's hands.

Action Ideas

Go to a Christian bookstore and take the time to look at the different books and devotionals for your daughter's age. Maybe you could find a book on dating!

Together listen to the tape *Adventures in Odyssey* "First Love" by Focus on the Family (audio cassette 1990).

Words to Memorize

Do not be yoked together with unbelievers.
2 Corinthians 6:14

Your Goal for This Week

_____

_____

_____

Closing Prayer

Heavenly Father, help me to prepare to follow Your will for my future. Guide me with Your wisdom in choosing a lifetime mate.

Section Three

GIFTS FROM THE HEART

Week Nine

OTHERS FIRST

Scripture Reading for This Week

2 Peter 1:5–9

For this very reason, make every effort to add to your faith goodness; and to goodness, knowledge; and to knowledge, self-control; and to self-control, perseverance; and to perseverance, godliness; and to godliness, brotherly kindness; and to brotherly kindness, love. For if you possess these qualities in increasing measure, they will keep you from being ineffective and unproductive in your knowledge of our Lord Jesus Christ. But if anyone does not have them, he is nearsighted and blind, and has forgotten that he has been cleansed from his past sins.

What words best describe the main point of these verses? Write them in the space below.

Daughter _____

Mom _____

Tell each other why you chose these words.

"Shannon," Mom called, "hurry up or you won't have time for breakfast."

Shannon shuffled into the kitchen and plopped down at the table.

"Morning, sweetie. Now, don't be late." Mom glanced at her daughter.

Shannon slouched sleepily over her cereal bowl. She didn't respond.

"By the way, Mom," Shannon said, resting her cheek against one hand with her elbow propped on the table, "the group is going to the mall this afternoon. OK?"

"I'm sorry, honey," Mom said as she turned toward her daughter. "I need you to pick up Joy from work as soon as class lets out. Today is payday and Joy is used to cashing her check right away." She waited, watching her daughter for signs of recognition.

Finally, the words began to sink in as Shannon sat up straight in her chair and stared wide-eyed at her mom. "I can't do it today, Mom. Any other time, I'd be glad to . . . but . . . just not today," Shannon stressed.

"I have no other choice, Shannon. I'll be in my meeting until 6:00 tonight. It just can't be helped."

"But I made plans to go to the mall with my friends. Please! Not today!" Shannon pleaded.

"I'm sorry, honey, but I need to count on you for this. . . . Your sister needs to count on you too."

Ouch! That arrow of guilt flew directly from Mom's lips and landed straight in the center of Shannon's heart.

Joy. Her big sister, Joy, was six years older and worked as a bagger at the neighborhood grocery. She hadn't missed a single day of work in the six months since she'd been working there.

That may not have seemed like much of an accomplishment for some eighteen year olds. But Joy and her family took great pride in this achievement because Joy had been born with Down's syndrome. Nothing came easily to her. Joy's life had been plagued by a continuous series of uncommon struggles.

Mom's small dose of guilt had worked. "OK, Mom," Shannon gave in with a whine. "But remember . . . you owe me!"

"Thanks, honey. And I know Joy will appreciate it too." She winked at Shannon. "She's always so eager to get to the bank with her paycheck."

❈ ❈ ❈

At 3:00 P.M. the school bell rang, dismissing classes for the day. Shannon made her apologies to her friends, said good-bye, and left to pick up Joy as she had promised. She found her waiting just inside the store by the automatic doors—her paycheck in one hand, her savings passbook in the other.

"Hi, Shannon," she greeted her sister with a shy smile. "Can we go to the bank now?" Her eyes were lit with eagerness.

"Sure. Let's go."

They walked the block and a half to the bank and found Joy's friend Mrs. Howland, who helped her each week with her deposit. Mrs. Howland said, "Hi, Joy. Who is this with you?"

"This is Shannon," Joy explained. "She's my sister."

"Hello, Shannon." Mrs. Howland took a deposit slip from the counter and began to fill in the blanks.

"Joy," Mrs. Howland said as she looked up, "do you want to deposit the usual amount in your student account?"

"Yes," she answered.

Within a few minutes, Mrs. Howland had all the paperwork completed and the two sisters were on their way home.

As they walked the four blocks toward home, Shannon's curiosity grew. Finally, she asked her sister, "What's a student account? Are you planning to go to school?"

"School's too hard for me," Joy answered. "Mama says I shouldn't worry about it, though, 'cause I was born to make people happy. That's why she named me Joy."

"So, what is the student account?" Shannon was really curious now.

Joy walked on in silence for a few seconds. Shannon could see her sister's face grow more serious as she thought about this question.

"It's for you," Joy whispered.

"For me?" Shannon was puzzled. "What do you mean it's for me?"

"It's for you to go to college," Joy confessed. "Mama said you're good in school, but she can't afford to send you to college."

"So every payday you put money in this account so I'll be able to go to college?" Shannon asked in disbelief.

"My Sunday school teacher says God likes it when we think of others first." Joy glanced sideways at her sister. "So I think of you first when I go to the bank."

Shannon just gawked in disbelief, staring at her sister's face like she was seeing it for the first time. Then she reached and brushed an unruly lock of hair away from Joy's face to reveal two broad-set, smiling eyes.

"Thank you," was all that Shannon could think to say as they turned the corner onto their street.

That day Joy gave her little sister a far greater gift than her contribution to a future college education. That day Shannon saw her sister in a new light—a sister with depth and a wisdom born of simplicity. Joy had also taught Shannon a simple but valuable lesson: Others first.

What the Story Says
Christ put our needs before His,
and He calls us to put others first.

Discussion Questions

1. Do you know anybody with Down's syndrome or another handicap? How do you treat the person? Do you respond the way Jesus would?

2. How did Shannon first respond to her mother's request to change her plans? Do you think you would have responded the same way?

3. What were some of the qualities that made Joy so special to her family? What are some of the special qualities of your brothers and sisters?

What Does the Bible Say?

Look up the following Scriptures and fill in the blanks.

Colossians 3:12
Therefore, as God's chosen people, holy and dearly loved, clothe yourselves with _____, _____, _____, _____ and _____.

How do we put on these qualities?

1 Corinthians 13:4
Love is _____, love is _____.

Ephesians 4:32
Be _____ and _____ to one
another, forgiving each other, just as in Christ God forgave you.

1 Thessalonians 5:15
Make sure that nobody pays back _____ for_____,
but always try to be kind to each other and to everyone else.

Romans 12:10
Be _____ to one another in brotherly love. Honor
one another above yourselves.

Looking Deeper

For Discussion:

Discuss and then list a few of the qualities we demonstrate when
we are thinking of others before ourselves.

_____

_____

_____

_____

_____

Compare your list with the following possibilities:

- Compassion
- Kindness
- Humility
- Gentleness
- Patience
- Devotion

Discuss and then list a few ways you can think of others first on a regular basis.

_____

_____

_____

_____

Compare your list to these possibilities:

- Visit someone who is lonely.
- Do something kind for someone else.
- Offer to do a chore you haven't been asked to do.
- Write a letter to a senior citizen to say you care.
- Try to be helpful and kind to the members of your family.
- Ask God to teach you how to love others.
- Tell someone how much you appreciate him or her.

List three reasons we should think of others before ourselves.

1. _____

2. _____

3. _____

Compare your ideas with those below:

- Christ put our needs before His own.
- The Bible tells us to.
- We will show Christ's love in our hearts.

Super! Now you have a plan. Try practicing it this week.

Action Ideas

Invite your daughter's teacher over for dinner or take her out to lunch.

Words to Memorize

Be devoted to one another in brotherly love.
Honor one another above yourselves.
Romans 12:10

Your Goal for This Week

_____

_____

_____

Closing Prayer

Lord, help me to be kind and caring to my family, friends, and others.

Week Ten

FORGIVE ME!

Scripture Reading for This Week

Psalm 130:1–7

Out of the depths I cry to you, O Lord; O Lord, hear my voice. Let your ears be attentive to my cry for mercy. If you, O Lord, kept a record of sins, O Lord, who could stand? But with you there is forgiveness; therefore you are feared.

I wait for the Lord, my soul waits, and in his word I put my hope. My soul waits for the Lord more than watchmen wait for the morning, more than watchmen wait for the morning.

O Israel, put your hope in the Lord, for with the Lord is unfailing love and with him is full redemption.

What words best describe the main point of these verses? Write them in the space below.

*Daughter*_____

Mom _____

Tell each other why you chose these words.

Little Women, the classic novel by Louisa May Alcott, tells the story of four sisters growing up during the Civil War. Their father had gone away to war to "stand up to the lions of injustice." The rest of the family—Marmee (their mother), Meg, Jo, Beth, and Amy—pulled together in his absence to survive a time of poverty and turmoil.

In one of the chapters, the youngest sister, Amy, wandered curiously into her older sisters' room on a Saturday afternoon while Meg and Jo prepared to go with their friend Laurie to the theater. Amy desperately wanted to go too. Cooped up in the house for several days with a cold, Amy craved excitement.

"I haven't got anything to do," Amy whined, "and am *so* lonely."

"You aren't invited," Meg told her kindly, as she tried to figure out some way they could take her anyway. But Jo let Amy know that she was not welcome to come. Laurie was ready to take them, and Jo was eager to leave her little sister behind, so they hurried down the stairs.

Amy followed her sisters with piercing eyes. Furious, she threatened, "You'll be sorry for this, Jo March!"

"Fiddlesticks!" Jo responded, slamming the door behind her.

Prone to violent outbursts when angered, both Jo and Amy possessed quick tempers. They had had many lively skirmishes over the years when Amy would tease Jo, and Jo would do things to irritate Amy—often exploding in battles between them.

Jo had a fiery spirit that was hard for her to control. She had continually found herself in trouble because of it. But Jo always repented quickly and recaptured Amy's affection.

After the play, Meg and Jo returned home to find Amy reading in the parlor, apparently still sulking. Amy said nothing but just stared at the pages of her book.

The next day Jo went to her desk and rummaged through

her papers. Since first learning to read and write, Jo had formed a habit of writing every night before getting into bed. For some time now, she'd been working on a collection of fairy tales she hoped to finish before her father returned home from the war. It was almost finished. The manuscript was irreplaceable—her only copy.

She searched the desk intently but didn't find her manuscript. Suddenly, alarm flashed across Jo's face. She spun around quickly and dashed from her room into Amy's.

Jo turned a look on Amy fierce enough to frighten a pit bull. "Amy, you've got it!"

"No, I haven't," she denied. But Jo kept asking her about it, until finally she said, "Scold as much as you like, you'll never see your silly old book again."

"Why not?"

"I burned it up."

Beside herself, Jo shook Amy, fists pounding her as she cried out, "You wicked, wicked girl! I never can write it again, and I'll never forgive you as long as I live."

Later that evening, Marmee stroked Jo's hair, trying to console her. "My dear," Marmee crooned, "don't let the sun go down upon your anger. Forgive each other, help each other, and begin again tomorrow." Marmee kissed the back of Jo's head, then glanced toward the doorway where Amy looked on sorrowfully.

But Jo wasn't ready to forgive, nor would she be comforted. The loss was just too great. "She don't deserve to be forgiven," Jo wailed.

By the following day, things had not improved. Jo decided to keep busy to avoid thinking about the lost manuscript. So she and her friend Laurie grabbed their skates and headed for the river. It might be their last chance to skate before spring melted the ice. Warmer weather had already formed a few soft spots on the surface.

As younger sisters often do, Amy tagged along uninvited. She raced to catch up with Jo and Laurie, but Jo carefully ignored her.

Jo and Laurie skated on, with Laurie taking the lead so he could look for soft spots in the ice. "Keep near the shore," he warned—"it isn't safe in the middle." But only Jo heard the warning. Within seconds, the crash of breaking ice, the splash of water, and an eerie cry pierced the stillness behind them. Jo's heart stood still in terror. She spun around in time to see Amy throw up her arms as she fell quickly below the ice.

With a swish, Laurie rushed past Jo shouting, "Bring a rail—quick, quick!"

He dropped to his knees and skidded to a stop beside the opening in the ice. Lying flat on the ice, he stretched his arms over to grab Amy's arm the next time it rose from the frigid darkness.

Jo pulled a rail from a broken fence and laid it across the hole for Amy to grasp, and together they pulled her from her dark tomb.

Safely back at home, Amy fell asleep in front of the fire, warming herself beneath a pile of blankets. The lost manuscript forgotten, Jo realized how close they had come to losing something far more precious—their dear little Amy. The reminder of Amy's irreplaceable value had restored forgiveness and peace.

"How could I be so wicked?" Jo said sadly, stroking Amy's wet hair. Amy opened her eyes and looked up at Jo with a smile that shot straight to her heart. The two girls hugged as they forgave each other.

What the Story Says

Forgiveness is a vital ingredient
in our relationships with others.

Discussion Questions

1. Did Jo have a good reason for being angry with Amy? Why?
2. What did Jo's anger almost cost her?
3. What lesson did Jo learn?

DEFINITION OF FORGIVENESS:
> To excuse for a fault or offense; to absolve; to stop feeling angry and resentful.

What Does the Bible Say?

Look up the following Scriptures and fill in the blanks.

Matthew 6:14–15
For if you _____ men when they sin against you, your heavenly Father will also _____ you. But if you do not _____ men their sins, your Father will not _____ your sins.

Luke 17:4
If he sins against you seven times in a day, and seven times comes back to you and says, "I repent," _____ him.

Matthew 18:21–22
Then Peter came to Jesus and asked, "Lord, how many _____ shall I forgive my brother when he _____ against me? Up to _____ times?" Jesus answered, "I tell you, not _____ times, but seventy-seven times."

What do you think Jesus meant by "seventy-seven times"?

Mark 11:25
And when you stand _____, if you hold anything
against anyone, forgive him, so that your Father in heaven may
_____ you your sins.

Colossians 3:13
Bear with each other and forgive whatever grievances you may
have against one another. _____ as the Lord _____
_____ you.

*We have all offended God our Father. We need to ask Him for
forgiveness. What do you need His forgiveness for today? What
do you need to forgive other people for?*

Luke 11:4
Forgive us our sins, for we also forgive _____ who sins
against us. And lead us not into temptation.

2 Chronicles 7:14
If my people, who are called by my name, will humble themselves and _____ and _____ my face and _____
from their wicked ways, then will I _____ from heaven and
will forgive their sin and will heal their land.

1 John 1:9
If we _____ our sins, he is faithful and just and
will forgive us our sins and _____ us from all unrighteousness.

What does it mean to "confess" our sins?

*Do you confess your sins to God? If not, ask your mom how to
do that.*

Word Scramble

1. fsecnos _____
2. beluhm _____
3. esfrgvionse _____

(For answers, see page 196.)

Looking Deeper

For Discussion:

Have you ever had a hard time forgiving someone who has done you wrong? How did that feel?

_____

_____

_____

For Mom:

Tell your daughter of a time when you were wronged. Tell her how you were able to eventually forgive and relinquish your resentment. Write down how you forgave.

_____

_____

_____

Mom, ask your daughter if she has ever asked God to forgive her sins and come into her heart. If so, when? Write down her answer.

_____

_____

_____

_____

For Daughter:

If not, do you want to do it right now? If you do, pray the following prayer together:

Lord Jesus, I am a sinner. Thank You for dying on the cross for me. Please forgive my sins and live in my heart forever. In Jesus' name, Amen.

For Discussion:

Discuss how you can _know_ that God forgives us when we ask.

_____

_____

_____

For Daughter:

Look at page 122 for a Scripture that promises God's forgiveness when we ask. Write it below.

_____

_____

_____

_____

_____

_____

_____

For Discussion:

Discuss and list below three reasons that we should forgive others.

1. _____

2. _____

3. _____

Compare your list to these possibilities:

- Because God tells us to.
- So that God will forgive us when we ask.
- To restore peace and mend our relationships.

For Mom:

Discuss with your daughter and then list below some tips that have helped you forgive others more easily.

_____

_____

_____

_____

For Discussion:

Discuss and identify three important personal qualities necessary to forgive. Write them below.

1. _____

2. _____

3. _____

Compare your list with the possibilities below.

- Obedience
- Compassion
- Love
- Gentleness
- Peacemaker
- Joy
- Patience
- A clear conscience
- Understanding
- Persistence

For Daughter:

With which of these qualities are you gifted? List them below.

_____

_____

_____

How can you exercise these qualities to practice forgiveness?

_____

_____

_____

Compare your ideas with those below:

- A clear conscience: Confess your sins every day, asking forgiveness from God as well as others.
- Love: If we focus on loving others, we won't notice their faults as much.

- Understanding: Remember how many times God and others have forgiven you.

All right! Now you have a plan. Try practicing it this week.

For Discussion:

Share your ideas and then list three ways you can practice forgiveness this week.

1. _____
2. _____
3. _____

Action Ideas

Take your dinner to the park . . . just the two of you! (Don't forget to take time for the swings and the jungle gym!)

Words to Memorize

If we confess our sins, he is faithful and just and will forgive us our sins and purify us from all unrighteousness.
1 John 1:9

Your Goal for This Week

_____

_____

_____

Closing Prayer

Lord, help me to run to You when I need forgiveness, and help me to forgive others.

Week Eleven

MIRROR, MIRROR

Scripture Reading for This Week

Matthew 23:27–28
You are like whitewashed tombs, which look beautiful on the outside but on the inside are full of dead men's bones and everything unclean. In the same way, on the outside you appear to people as righteous but on the inside you are full of hypocrisy and wickedness.

1 Peter 3:3–4
Your beauty should not come from outward adornment, such as braided hair and the wearing of gold jewelry and fine clothes. Instead, it should be that of your inner self, the unfading beauty of a gentle and quiet spirit, which is of great worth in God's sight.

What words best describe the main point of these verses? Write them in the space below.

*Daughter*_____

Mom _____

Tell each other why you chose these words.

Catherine pushed open the front door, stepped inside, and slammed it shut behind her. Her shoulders sloped slightly forward in gloomy resignation; a dark storm had settled over her face. As she made her way down the hall toward her bedroom, she passed the kitchen, where her mom looked up from washing salad greens for dinner and asked, "How was school?"

Catherine walked by without a word. When she reached her room, she closed the door, dropped her backpack onto the floor, and threw herself face down across the bed.

"I'm never going back to that lousy school!" she promised herself, glaring at the carpet.

A knock at the door interrupted Catherine's thoughts. "Who is it?" she muttered.

"It's Mom, Cath. Can I come in?"

"I guess."

Her mother opened the door and stepped inside the room. "Hey, you OK?" She walked over to the bed and sat on the edge. "You look as if you've lost your best friend."

Catherine was relieved by her mom's presence, but she continued staring at the floor. "I don't have any friends to lose," she mumbled as if it didn't matter anyway.

"What about Lisa? I thought Lisa was your best friend."

At the sound of Lisa's name, Catherine rolled over and sat upright, facing her mom. "I thought she was too!" The words burst from her lips. "Lisa's not _my_ friend!" Catherine spouted.

"What happened?" Mom asked.

"Well . . . the thing is . . . you see . . ." Catherine tried to find the words. She crossed her legs Indian style and stared down at her fidgeting fingers. "You see, Lisa said I was fat and that I would look better if I lost weight," she managed. "And she just _had_ to say it in front of all our friends . . ." Catherine's voice trailed off. "They all thought it was *so* funny." A tear escaped Catherine's eye and spilled onto her cheek.

"That was a mean thing to do," Mom defended her daughter's feelings.

"But she's right, Mom. I *am* fat!" Catherine clutched her tummy. "I already know it. She doesn't have to remind me!"

"But, Cath, you're *not* fat," Mom reached a hand up to brush a tear from her daughter's face.

Mom understood how Catherine felt. She could remember what it felt like to be eleven years old. Catherine's body had started to change. Where once had been a flat chest, breasts were beginning to form. Her waist had not yet defined itself, and she retained a tiny pouch of baby fat around her midriff that would be gone within a year. She no longer had the body of a little girl, but she was not yet a woman.

Mom patted her daughter's knee. "Your body is changing as you grow, Cath. Your figure will continue to change over the next few years as you become a young woman. But you are perfect just the way you are." Mom gave her knee a squeeze. "And you're *not* fat!"

"You *have* to say that. You're my mom," Catherine discounted her mom's words.

"Some of the most beautiful women in the world hate *something* about their looks."

"Really?"

"Really," Mom assured her. "And even your beautiful Aunt Chris, who everyone says you take after . . . well, ask her sometime how she felt about her looks at your age."

Mom grabbed her daughter and pulled her down on the bed. "OK, let's snuggle," she said as they settled in and Catherine found her favorite spot to cuddle, resting her head in the crook of Mom's warm arm.

"Let me tell you about Aunt Chris," Mom said. "You might be really surprised with something she struggled with at your age.

"You have seen how tall Aunt Chris is—well, just think of being almost that tall and in the seventh grade. At school one boy called her Jolly Green Giant every day as she walked into the cafeteria. You can imagine how awkward she felt and how embarrassed she was in front of her friends.

"There were times she looked into the mirror and thought she looked like a tall, gawky giraffe. All she could see were her long legs. She never noticed her beautiful eyes that sparkled when she smiled and talked with her friends.

"The long legs that embarrassed Aunt Chris in seventh grade were the same long legs that helped her to become an all-star basketball player in high school.

"Cath, did you know if you asked eight out of ten teenagers, there would be at least one major thing they did not like about the way they looked?"

"So I shouldn't be upset about being called fat?" Catherine asked honestly.

"Of course you're going to care what others think of you. Just try not to take it too seriously." Mom gave her daughter a squeeze. "What others think isn't as important as what you think of yourself. If you feel your value lies in being merely decorative, I fear that someday you might find yourself believing that's all you really are. Time erodes physical beauty. But what it cannot diminish is the uniqueness of who you are: your humor, your kindness, and your moral courage. These are the qualities I cherish most in you." Mom kissed Catherine's forehead.

"Thanks, Mom."

What the Story Says

Be careful not to drown in the obsession of self
and the pursuit of physical beauty. And don't focus
so much on the physical features you dislike
that you miss the ones that are good!

Discussion Questions

1. Do you feel pressure from your friends, yourself, or other sources to look a certain way?

2. Which of your physical characteristics are you not totally comfortable with? How does this affect the way you feel about yourself?

3. What are some things that are more important than the way you look?

DEFINITION OF OBSESSION:
> A persistent, disturbing preoccupation with an unreasonable idea or feeling.

DEFINITION OF SELF-CENTERED:
> Concerned solely with one's own desires, needs, and interests.

What Does the Bible Say?

Look up the following Scriptures and fill in the blanks.

John 7:24
Stop _____ by mere appearances, and make a
right judgment.

Galatians 2:6
God does _____ judge by external appearance.

What do you think God does *judge by?*

1 Samuel 16:7
The Lord does not look at the things man looks at. Man looks at
the _____ appearance, but the Lord looks at the

_____.

Proverbs 31:30
Charm is _____, and beauty is _____;
but a woman who fears the Lord is to be praised.

Looking Deeper

For Mom:

Which physical characteristics made you feel inadequate when
you were your daughter's age? Discuss them and then list them
below.

_____

_____

_____

For Discussion:

Discuss places this pressure to be physically perfect comes from
and list them.

_____

_____

_____

Compare your list to these possibilities:

- Television commercials.
- Magazines.
- The "Hollywood" mind-set.
- Peers.
- Friends and relatives who only notice what they can see about you.
- The obvious "favors" reserved for only the beautiful and popular people.

For Mom:

Discuss with your daughter and then list below some of the tips that have helped you gain perspective about your looks.

_____

_____

_____

_____

_____

Identify and discuss three qualities your daughter possesses that do not relate to her physical beauty. Write them below.

1. _____

2. _____

3. _____

Compare these qualities with those below. The possibilities are limitless.

1. A sense of humor
2. Honesty
3. A sense of fairness
4. Gentleness
5. Kindness
6. Generosity
7. Faith
8. An attitude of optimism
9. Compassion
10. A sharp mind
11. Wisdom
12. Loyalty
13. Shrewdness
14. Trustworthiness
15. A heart for God

For Daughter:

On which areas in the list above would you be graded "needs improvement"? Which of those would you like to work on?

_____

_____

_____

_____

Discuss and write how you can develop these qualities on a daily basis to develop your inner beauty.

_____

_____

_____

_____

Compare your ideas with those below:

- Write down five or six verses about beauty that you'd like to memorize over the next few weeks. Write them on an index card and tape the card to your mirror.
- Identify three things that happened this week that pressured you to think of yourself as merely decorative.
- On a sheet of paper, make a list of your finest inner qualities and carry it with you. Look for ways to use these qualities on a daily basis. Identify three weaknesses as well.

Super! Now you have a plan. Try practicing it this week.

For Discussion:

Discuss your ideas with each other and list three ways you can resist the temptation to be self-centered.

1. _____

2. _____

3. _____

Compare the following ideas with yours:

- Make it a priority to think of others every day.
- Take time this week to do something kind for someone else.
- Send a card to someone who needs encouragement or the hand of friendship.

Combine the two lists and you have your plan. Follow through with these ideas this week.

Action Ideas

Introduce your daughter to Christian contemporary music—or if she has a favorite Christian singer, make up your own exercise routine. Make it an aerobic night of fun!

Words to Memorize

Man looks at the outward appearance,
but the Lord looks at the heart.
1 Samuel 16:7

Your Goal for This Week

_____

_____

_____

Closing Prayer

Heavenly Father, help me to focus my attention on becoming more like You and developing my inner beauty.

Week Twelve

THE HIDING PLACE

Scripture Reading for This Week

Luke 12:22–34

Then Jesus said to his disciples: "Therefore I tell you, do not worry about your life, what you will eat; or about your body, what you will wear. Life is more than food, and the body more than clothes. Consider the ravens: They do not sow or reap, they have no storeroom or barn; yet God feeds them. And how much more valuable you are than birds! Who of you by worrying can add a single hour to his life? Since you cannot do this very little thing, why do you worry about the rest?

"Consider how the lilies grow. They do not labor or spin. Yet I tell you, not even Solomon in all his splendor was dressed like one of these. If that is how God clothes the grass of the field, which is here today, and tomorrow is thrown into the fire, how much more will he clothe you, O you of little faith! And do not set your heart on what you will eat or drink; do not worry about it. For the pagan world runs after all such things, and your Father knows that you need them. But seek his kingdom, and these things will be given to you as well.

"Do not be afraid, little flock, for your Father has been pleased to give you the kingdom. Sell your possessions and give to the poor. Provide purses for yourselves that will not wear out, a treasure in heaven that will not be exhausted, where no thief comes near and no moth destroys. For where your treasure is, there your heart will be also."

What words best describe the main point of these verses? Write them in the space below.

Daughter _____

Mom _____

Tell each other why you chose these words.

$\mathcal{I}$f you asked your grandparents or other older people about World War II, they would quickly tell you stories of their experiences and how the war affected them. In 1944 a giant shadow was cast over most of the world as German armies marched across Europe, seizing everything in their pathway. Along the way, the Nazis arrested whole communities of Jews—simply because they were Jewish. The Germans also confiscated everything they owned. These people were torn from their homes, and separated from their families, and locked up in savage death camps. Millions of them starved or were executed.

In its sweep across Europe, Germany occupied the tiny country of Holland. Violence against Jews in Holland was increasing every day. Amid the nightmare of hatred and fear, groups of compassionate and courageous citizens decided to do something to help the Jews. They organized to offer shelter to these refugees and help them escape certain death.

The ten Boom family joined the Dutch resistance. The family's charming old watch shop and home, with their odd angles and unmatched walls, disguised a secret, third-floor room—a hiding place where refugees could find shelter until an escape plan was arranged.

But their secret was discovered. On February 28, 1944, life as the ten Boom family had known it ended when the Gestapo (the German police) burst into their home and arrested the family.

The giant shadow fell over the ten Boom household, and clouds began to gather that would eventually block out the sun completely. In the darkness nobody guessed how their lives would change forever.

※ ※ ※

Several weeks after the Gestapo raid on their home, Corrie ten Boom lay in her prison cell, tossing and turning on a narrow cot that was now her bed, trying in vain to find a position where her body didn't hurt.

The cell was deep and narrow, scarcely wider than the door. Against the wall, a narrow metal cot with a filthy straw mat made her bed. The smell of sour straw hung thick in the air. Two hooks on the wall held her coat and hat. Corrie's only other belongings were a needle and thread, a couple of safety pins, and four small booklets, each containing one of the Gospels—Matthew, Mark, Luke, and John. She felt fortunate to have these things, though, and kept her treasures hidden in a ragged pillow slip under her cot.

Even though Corrie was young at heart, she was not a young woman. Corrie had just turned fifty-two years old. Neither she nor her older sister, Betsie, had married. Both had lived their entire lives in their father's home.

During the first few days of her imprisonment, Corrie remained in a constant state of panic about her father and Betsie. She fretted over whether Father would be able to eat the awful food, and she wondered if Betsie's condition was as bad as her own.

Eventually, though, Corrie was forced to find ways to keep her mind distracted from these concerns that threatened to overwhelm her.

Corrie was in solitary confinement. She spent her days totally alone. The closest she came to human contact was when the guard pushed open a small compartment in the door to give her a steaming bowl of watery gray porridge. A little while later, the bowl would be collected and the opening in the door slammed shut. Corrie ached for human touch—or even the sight of another human face.

She learned to fear the loneliness and boredom that was now a part of every day. As the weeks went by, she developed a few daily rituals to help break the monotony and distract her from her loneliness.

Corrie's cell had one attractive feature—a window. Although it was too high to see anything except the sky through it, Corrie would stare for hours at that piece of sky. And best of all, each day for about an hour a stream of sunlight burst through the small window and into the dark cell. When this happened, Corrie would press her back against the wall of her cell to catch the sunshine on her face. As the sun made its way across the sky, Corrie inched along the wall to keep the light on her face until, finally, she would perch tiptoe on the cot to relish the last few warm rays.

What helped her most, though, was her daily reading of the Gospels. In them the whole magnificent drama of salvation unfolded, and over time her perspective on her circumstances gradually began to change. She began to wonder if what had happened to her was accidental at all. Could it be part of God's plan? After all, to human eyes hadn't Jesus been utterly defeated as well?

Each night before Corrie lay down to sleep, she marked off one more day on the calendar she had scratched on the wall over her cot. Beneath the calendar she had listed significant events and their dates. Those were:

February 28, 1944	Arrested
February 29, 1944	Transport to Scheveningen
March 16, 1944	Beginning of Solitary
April 15, 1944	My Birthday in Prison

Then Corrie would lie down on her cot to pray. Every day of her life had ended this way. At home each evening, everyone would gather around her father for evening prayers. With a far-away wistfulness in his eyes, he would recite from memory, "You are my hiding place and my shield: I hope in your word. Hold me up, and I will be safe." And then that deep steady voice would relinquish the care of his loved ones to God in prayer.

Those days, just months ago, now seemed like another lifetime to Corrie.

Eventually, Corrie would drop off to sleep nurturing fond thoughts of her faraway family and memories of the life they had known before the war. These scenes graced her restless slumber and carried her through the fearful hours of nighttime.

❦ ❦ ❦

Days at the ten Boom home had been filled with a flurry of people and activities, because the door was always open to anyone who needed a helping hand. In addition to Mother and Father, four children, and an assortment of aunts, numerous houseguests shared the home. In the ten Boom house, hospitality could always be found.

In the evenings the whole household gathered together in the front room. Guests brought their flutes or violins. Since each member of the family sang or played an instrument, they made quite an orchestra gathered around the upright piano. These evenings had always been very happy with lots of fun and laughter . . . and lots of hot coffee.

But that was before the war.

While the kids were growing up, the best moment in every day had been when Father came up to tuck them into bed. None of them ever fell asleep until he had arranged the blankets in his special way and laid his hand for a moment on each head.

Corrie remembered one particular night after a neighbor's baby had died. She had been so upset all day that she hadn't eaten a thing. When her father stepped into her room that night, Corrie burst into tears and blurted out, "I need you! You can't die! You can't!"

Her father sat down on the edge of her bed. "Corrie," he spoke gently, "when you and I go to Amsterdam—when do I give you your ticket?"

Corrie sniffed a few times, thinking about his question. "Why, just before we get on the train," she answered.

"Exactly. And our wise Father in heaven knows when we're going to need things, too. Don't run out ahead of Him, Corrie. When the time comes that some of us will have to die, you will look into your heart and find the strength you need—just in time."

She did not know then as she listened to her father's footsteps winding back down the stairs that he had given her more than the key to that hard moment. He had put into her heart the secret that would get her through the dark hours years later.

She had lived in her tiny prison cell for more than two months when one day the compartment in her door banged open and shut again with a single motion. Corrie heard something drop to the concrete. Her eyes squinted, searching the shadows. Then she spotted it. There on the floor of the cell lay an envelope. She sprang forward and picked it up with trembling hands. She recognized the handwriting of her older sister Nollie.

Her first letter from home!

For a moment, she just held the envelope in her hands and studied it. She could tell that the censors had opened the envelope and kept it for some time because the postmark was several weeks old.

Corrie pinched open the envelope, carefully unfolded the letter, and read:

"Corrie, can you be very brave?"

A voice inside her screamed *No! No, I can't be brave!* But she forced her eyes to keep reading.

"I have news that is very hard to write you. Father survived his arrest by only ten days. He is now with the Lord. . . ."

She crouched near the floor. *Father . . . Father gone.* The words began to sink in as she read the rest of the letter. Nollie had no details, not how or where he had died, not even where he was buried.

Corrie returned to her cot and lay thinking for a long time about her father. A Scripture verse she had read earlier in the day kept popping into her mind. It was from John 14 where Jesus was comforting His disciples. She opened her booklet of John and read it again:

> Let not your heart be troubled: ye believe in God, believe also in me. In my Father's house are many mansions: if it were not so, I would have told you. I go to prepare a place for you. And if I go and prepare a place for you, I will come again, and receive you unto myself; that where I am, there ye may be also (KJV).

Corrie knew her dear father was with Jesus. She got up and pulled her cot away from the wall. Below the calendar she scratched another date:

March 9, 1944   Father Released

And now I will have to search deep in my own heart for the strength to get through this time, she thought to herself. Father had promised that God would give it "just in time."

Corrie spent eight more months in prison and always found what she needed "just in time." And in the hiding place of God's love, Corrie found refuge and discovered a profound comfort: No pit is so deep that the love of God is not deeper still!

What the Story Says

When tragedy strikes, there is a hiding place
where we can take refuge in God's love.

Discussion Questions

1. What if Corrie were your grandmother? Imagine your own grandmother locked up and forced to sleep on rotten straw in a cell. How would you feel?
2. How did Corrie encourage herself while she was in the prison camp?
3. Can you imagine being in a tough situation like Corrie? Do you think your own trust in Christ would get you through it?

DEFINITION OF REFUGE:
 Shelter or protection from danger.

What Does the Bible Say?

Look up the following Scriptures and fill in the blanks.

Psalm 32:7
You are my _____; you will _____
me from trouble and surround me with songs of _____.

Psalm 17:8
Keep me as the apple of your eye; _____ me in the _____
_____ of your wings.

Psalm 27:5
For in the day of trouble he will keep me _____ in his
dwelling; he will hide me in the _____ of his tabernacle and set me high upon a _____.

Psalm 143:9
Rescue me from my enemies, O Lord, for I _____
myself in you.

Psalm 62:1
My soul finds rest in _____ alone; my salvation
comes from him.

*Where do you look when you need to be rescued from difficul-
ties?*

Psalm 62:5
Find rest, O my soul, in God alone; my _____ comes
from him.

Psalm 62:8
_____ in him at all times, O people; pour out
your hearts to him, for God is our _____.

Looking Deeper

For Discussion:

What does a refuge provide? Make a list below.

_____

_____

_____

Compare your list to these possibilities:

- Safety and security
- Stability
- Encouragement
- Fulfillment
- Comfort
- Peace
- Hope
- Confidence
- Purpose
- Rest

For Daughter:

Have you ever had an experience where you felt you needed a refuge . . . a hiding place? Tell your mom about it. Where did you look for refuge?

_____

_____

_____

Compare your list to the following possibilities:

- Friends
- Family
- Escape in TV, music, or fun

- A relationship with God
- Being alone

For Mom:

Tell your daughter of a time in your life when your hiding place was found in Christ. Write a summary of that below.

_____

_____

_____

_____

For Daughter:

You will probably never have to face anything as tough as Corrie did, but what dangers might you face where you will need to "hide" in God's love?

_____

_____

_____

_____

How can you prepare yourself so that when a crisis strikes you will know how to find comfort in the hiding place of God's love?

_____

_____

_____

_____

Compare your ideas to the possibilities below:

- Get to know God by reading His Word.
- Practice trusting God in the small problems of life.
- Memorize God's promises to protect you.

Super! Now you have a plan. Try practicing it this week.

Action Ideas

If you haven't already seen the movie *The Hiding Place* about Corrie ten Boom's life, your church library may have a video copy for you to borrow, or your local Christian bookstore may have it for you to rent. Choose some fun snacks and watch the movie together.

Words to Memorize

The Lord is my strength and my shield;
my heart trusts in him, and I am helped.
Psalm 28:7

Your Goal for This Week

_____

_____

_____

Closing Prayer

Lord, You have personally numbered my days on this earth. Help me to learn to trust You with my life.

Section Four

COMMITMENT IS COOL

Week Thirteen

FOLLOW ME

Scripture Reading for This Week

John 10:3, 14–15, 27
   The watchman opens the gate for him, and the sheep listen to his voice. He calls his own sheep by name and leads them out. . . .
   I am the good shepherd; I know my sheep and my sheep know me—just as the Father knows me and I know the Father—and I lay down my life for the sheep. . . .
   My sheep listen to my voice; I know them, and they follow me.

What words best describe the main point of these verses? Write them in the space below.

*Daughter*_____

Mom _____

Tell each other why you chose these words.

*O*nce upon a time, on the rocky hillsides of a far-off land, a shepherd owned a flock of one hundred sheep that he loved dearly. He was a kind and attentive shepherd who knew each of his sheep by name. Always on the lookout for predators that might attack the flock, he carefully tended his flock day and night and made a home for them on a summit where he could guard them from danger.

A stream ran from the higher mountains into the valley where the shepherd guided his flock each day for water. Early in the morning he would lead them down the treacherous slopes of the hillside to the valley below, where they would spend most of the day basking in sunshine, drinking from the stream, and nibbling lazily on tender blades of grass.

Then before nightfall, the shepherd would carefully lead his flock back up the pathway, along the dangerous cliffs, and onto the safety of the summit.

The sheep tried to stay close together, and they took comfort in the familiar sound of their shepherd's voice as he sang to them and spoke encouragingly along the way. "Follow me, now. . . . Follow me," he would call to them as they made their way home.

A lamb named Jingles lived in the flock along with her mother and her twin sister, Daisy. Jingles had a reputation for "doing her own thing." Mama said she had been like that since the day she was born and could stand on all four legs. She had gotten the name "Jingles" because she wandered from the flock so many times that the shepherd tied a leather strap with a bell around her neck so he could hear her. She jingled every time she took a step.

"Now stay close, girls," Mama bleated to Daisy and Jingles as they made their way back home after a long spring day in the valley.

"OK, Mama," Daisy answered, moving in closer to her mother.

"Oh, Mama," Jingles complained. "You never let me stop to play."

"It's growing dark," Mama warned. "There's no time to play until after we get back home."

But something had caught Jingles's attention and she hardly heard her mother.

A tiny hummingbird buzzed above Jingles's head and dropped low to hover over a patch of wildflowers just a few feet away. Jingles froze and stood absolutely still for several moments as she watched the bird dance in midair over the flowers. *What a perfect chance for a little fun!* Jingles thought as she crept closer.

Pounce! She jumped toward the bird. But the hummingbird simply flew to another patch of flowers a bit farther away from Jingles.

Fascinated, Jingles followed the bird and chased it as it moved from flower to flower. Finally, though, the hummingbird grew tired of the pesky lamb and suddenly rose high into the sky and disappeared.

The fun over, Jingles turned to rejoin Mama and Daisy. But the flock was nowhere in sight. "Mama, where are you?" Jingles bleated into the darkening sky. She stretched her head as tall as she could reach, looking as far as she could to see any sign of the shepherd's head. Then she stood very still, straining to hear the faint sound of his voice.

Nothing!

Then suddenly, a deep growl came from behind a bush.

"What's that?" Jingles jumped back, startled by the unfamiliar sound. She stood and stared at the rustling bush.

A mountain lion stepped from behind the bush and looked right at Jingles with his hungry eyes. *Dinner!* His eyes sparkled as he surveyed the situation.

The giant cat sauntered in a circle around Jingles, who was now trembling in terror. She bleated her distress into the wind. But no one except the lion heard. The little lamb was hardly a challenge for him to capture. It was almost too good to be true.

The lion pounced. The helpless lamb jumped out of his way just as the cat leaped. The claws on its front paws snared small shreds of wool as she tumbled over the edge of the cliff. She fell a few feet and then suddenly stopped. She was safe for now, but she pictured him tossing her around like a moth caught in its giant paws, his sharp claws cutting deeply into her flesh, leaving blood stains on her soft wool.

"Help," she bleated.

But no one except the lion heard.

Her wool had caught on something—a branch growing out of the side of the cliff. Jingles just dangled there flailing tiny legs wildly to get free, not realizing she would fall to the rocky canyon far below if she freed herself. The bell around her neck jangled frantically.

Above her head, Jingles could see the hungry face of the lion peering over the edge at her. He reached a front paw down to snag her, but she was just out of his reach. He tried with the other front paw but couldn't quite reach the lamb without falling into the same predicament.

Jingles just hung there bawling and jangling.

Meanwhile, the shepherd had noticed that Jingles was missing. He quickly led his flock to the safety of the summit, then immediately turned and ran in search of the little lost lamb. Momentarily, he paused to listen for a cry. Or the jingle of a bell.

Nothing.

He ran on ahead for a ways, then stopped again to listen.

Still nothing.

His feet moved swiftly through the brush, looking, listening, searching for any sign of Jingles.

Suddenly, he stopped and stood very still. He had heard something. A small sound at first, caught by the wind. Then, there it was again. Yes, he recognized the cries of his little lost lamb. She was in danger. He ran toward the sound, but now he called out to the lamb as he ran. "I am coming," he hollered. "I am coming."

Jingles heard the familiar sound of her shepherd's voice and felt a spark of hope. He would save her.

At the sound of the shepherd, the lion retreated, deciding to take his plans for dinner somewhere else.

When the shepherd reached the edge of the cliff, he bent down low, reached over the side of the cliff, and tenderly grabbed hold of Jingles. He lifted the bruised and trembling lamb close to his chest and cradled her there for a few moments. "I've got you, now," he said. "You'll be OK."

Jingles looked up into his kind face. She felt safe again. "Ba-a-a-a-a-a-a," she offered her thanks.

"There, now," the shepherd stroked the back of her head, "you'll be all right now." Then he set her down on the ground at his feet. "Let's go home," he said.

And with great joy they began their trek back to the flock. All the while the shepherd gently called to Jingles over his shoulder, "Follow me, now," he said. "Follow me."

What the Story Says

Jesus calls us to listen to His voice and follow Him.

Discussion Questions

1. Did Jingles listen to her mother and the shepherd? What were they telling her?

2. Why do you think she didn't pay attention to their warnings?

3. Are you ever tempted to ignore warnings from your parents?

What Does the Bible Say?

Look up the following Scriptures and fill in the blanks.

Luke 15:7
I tell you that in the same way there will be more rejoicing in heaven over one _____ who repents than over ninety-nine _____ persons who do not need to repent.

Leviticus 19:37
Keep all my _____ and all my _____ and follow them. I am the Lord.

Luke 9:23
Then he said to them all: "If _____ would come after me, he must _____ himself and take up his cross daily and follow me."

What does it mean to "deny" yourself and take up your "cross"?

John 10:3–4
He calls his own sheep by _____ and leads them out. When he has brought out all his own, he goes on ahead of them, and his sheep _____ him because they know his voice.

John 10:14–15
I am the good shepherd; I _____ my sheep and my sheep _____ me—just as the Father knows me and I know the Father—and I lay down my life for the sheep.

John 10:27–28
My sheep _____ to my voice; I know them, and they _____ me. I give them eternal life, and they shall never

perish; no one can snatch them out of my hand.

1 Peter 2:25
For you were like _____ going astray, but now you have
returned to the _____ and Overseer of your souls.

Looking Deeper

For Discussion:

What are some of the ways you can wander away from Jesus?

_____

_____

_____

_____

_____

_____

Compare your answers to the following possibilities:

- By becoming distracted by other things.
- By following after something that is not God's will.
- By forgetting to confess sin.

What should you do when you discover you have wandered away
from God? How can you find your way back?

_____

_____

_____

_____

Compare your list to these possibilities:

- Repent and ask God for forgiveness.
- Identify what led you away from God and get rid of it.
- Remember to listen for the Shepherd's voice.

For Mom:

Was there a time when you wandered away from the Lord? Tell your daughter about it, and discuss some of the things that have helped you to keep following Jesus. Write them below.

_____

_____

_____

_____

_____

For Daughter:

Discuss and identify several things that might come up in the next five years to distract you from following Jesus. Write them below.

_____

_____

_____

_____

_____

What might you do to prepare yourself to keep from being distracted by other things and turning away from Jesus?

_____

_____

_____

Compare your ideas with those below:

- Spend time each day in prayer and Bible study.
- Practice listening for the voice of your Shepherd.
- Be sure to keep your heart pure. When you sin, immediately confess that sin and ask God's forgiveness.

All right! Now you have a plan. Try practicing it this week.

Action Ideas

Go to the batting cages or go out for ice cream.

Words to Memorize

I am the good shepherd. The good
shepherd lays down his life for the sheep.
John 10:11

Your Goal for This Week

_____

_____

_____

Closing Prayer

Dear Lord, help me to listen to Your voice and follow You.

Week Fourteen

ARE YOU COMMITTED?

Scripture Reading for This Week

Mark 8:34–38

Then he called the crowd to him along with his disciples and said: "If anyone would come after me, he must deny himself and take up his cross and follow me. For whoever wants to save his life will lose it, but whoever loses his life for me and for the gospel will save it. What good is it for a man to gain the whole world, yet forfeit his soul? Or what can a man give in exchange for his soul? If anyone is ashamed of me and my words in this adulterous and sinful generation, the Son of Man will be ashamed of him when he comes in his Father's glory with the holy angels."

$\mathscr{I}$t had been almost two hundred years since Christ's crucifixion. Christians from Rome had brought the gospel to North Africa, and many people had accepted Christ.

Young Vibia Perpetua was one of those new believers, and on a warm spring day she and her husband joined other Christians beside a lake where they would be baptized. Vibia nestled their newborn son in one arm as she and her husband watched silently and waited for their turn to enter the water, publicly professing their faith in Christ.

Twenty-two years old, beautiful, of noble birth, and well educated, Vibia's ties with the world were already strong. She probably didn't know what her commitment to Christ would cost her.

❧ ❧ ❧

Vibia and her husband lived in North Africa, where prejudice and superstition against Christians had swept the land. The frightened pagans demanded laws they could use against Christians. Responding to pressure from a few influential people, the Roman emperor issued a law making it illegal to become a Christian. Roman Procurator Hilarianus fanatically enforced this new law in North Africa.

So the infant church of Christ entered the martyr age. Men, women, and children were torn from their homes, judged to be dangerous citizens, and condemned to die. The jails were full of them, and executions took place daily. Certain Christians were set aside for show because in those days killing had become a spectator sport. Defenseless Christians going to battle with wild beasts and armed gladiators quickly became the favorite Roman pastime.

In spite of this persecution, spiritual passion grew and the gospel spread. Small groups of believers met secretly in homes to worship together. Vibia and her husband joined their group of new believers each week.

Inside the neighborhoods spies lurked, reporting the names of those who gathered. Rumors spread of Vibia's baptism, and she and her husband were listed among the new Christians.

Early one morning guards converged on Vibia's home. They burst through the front door; grabbed Vibia, her husband, and their newborn baby; and ushered them to the proconsul.

The blush of sleep had not yet left Vibia's face, but it began to pale as the guards rushed them into the great judgment hall and before the seat of the proconsul. First to be thrust to the center of the room, Vibia stood alone to face her accuser.

She trembled, staring down at the marble floor beneath her. The proconsul glared at the beautiful girl who stood before him. "Young woman, they say you are a Christian," his voice thundered.

Vibia raised her face slightly to meet his eyes.

"Are you a Christian?" he demanded.

"Yes, I am a Christian," Vibia confessed shyly.

"Come now, child," he ordered, "believe what you like, but do what I tell you; deny your faith and worship the statue of our great emperor."

"I can't do that," Vibia replied, looking straight into the governor's eyes—more confident now. "I'm a Christian."

"Don't waste my time, foolish girl," he snapped. "Do what I say!"

Vibia's husband broke loose from the guard's grasp and bolted toward her. Guards jumped him. "Vibia, you will kill yourself, and you will kill me too," he pleaded, reaching toward her as the guards dragged him back to one side.

Vibia watched helplessly. Tears spilled from her eyes and a sob caught in her throat. "I will do anything you ask me to do except this. My Lord is my Master."

Turning again to face the governor, she repeated, "I am a Christian; I cannot do that."

Though speechless in the face of such a fearless confession, the proconsul had no choice but to find Vibia guilty of disloyalty to the emperor.

Her husband, unable to endure such a grave test of his young faith, quickly stepped forward to renounce Christianity. Vibia's eyes widened as she watched him bow before the altar of the emperor, then run sobbing from the amphitheater.

The guards threw Vibia into prison, along with other members of her tiny church.

"I was very much afraid," Vibia wrote that night in her diary, "because I had never experienced such gloom. [I also experienced] fearful heat because of the crowd and from the jostling of the soldiers! Finally I was racked with anxiety for my infant."

That night Vibia's baby was brought to her for the last time. She cuddled her tiny son as she soothed him with a lullaby and committed his future to her Father in heaven. She thought of her dear husband also, asking God to guide him down the treacherous path of questioning and grief.

Vibia and her friends prepared to die—now concerned only with their own worthiness to suffer for Christ. For their last meal, instead of the feast usually given to condemned prisoners, they shared an *agape*—a simple religious meal, celebrating Christ's death and their love for each other. And they prayed they would have the courage to stand in the face of death.

The next day guards led Vibia and the other Christians to a huge amphitheater. First, Procurator Hilarianus would question them—offering them one more opportunity to save their lives. Hilarianus perched on the judgment seat, positioned on a platform opposite stone bleachers that hosted a bloodthirsty crowd. Vibia stood alone in the center of the platform as the crowd screamed, "Throw them to the beasts!"

"Are you a Christian?" Hilarianus shouted over the noisy crowd.

"I am," Vibia confirmed. "I cannot forsake my faith for freedom. I *will* not do it, for Christ is my life, and death to me is gain."

After questioning each of the Christians, Hilarianus signaled the executioners, who herded Vibia and her friends to the entrance of the arena to await their turn for execution.

Hunters released a leopard, a bear, and a wild boar into the arena. Vibia and her friends huddled together and comforted each other with prayers and the reminder that soon they would be in the arms of their Lord.

They gathered their courage and, with faces radiating an unseen Presence, began singing a psalm. Wearing a simple tunic and with her long braids cascading over her shoulders, Vibia marched into the arena.

Vibia met her death on a March day in 203 A.D. Assisted by wild animals and gladiators' swords, she and her friends stepped into the loving arms of their Lord.

The blood and tears of these lovers of Christ were not wasted, though. They moistened the ground into which new seed would fall and produce a harvest for Christ's kingdom. Christianity continued to grow, drawing people to the faith that produced such devotion.

In her young life, Vibia experienced a dramatic encounter with Christ that became more important than life itself. She learned a lesson that requires a lifetime of lessons for most of us. Vibia learned that Christ is life and to die for Him is gain.

What the Story Says

Following Christ will always cost us something,
but Christ gives us the strength we need.

Discussion Questions

1. What does it mean to be committed to Christ?

2. How much of our lives should we be willing to give to God?

3. Why do you think Vibia was willing to give even her life?

DEFINITION OF COMMITMENT:
A promise, an obligation.

What Does the Bible Say?

Look up the following Scriptures and fill in the blanks.

Matthew 16:24–25
If anyone would come after me, he must _____ himself and take up his cross and follow me. For whoever wants to _____ his life will lose it, but whoever loses his life for me will _____ it.

John 15:8
This is to my Father's _____, that you bear much fruit.

What does it mean to bear fruit?

Mark 8:36
What good is it for a man to _____ the whole world, yet forfeit his _____?

Galatians 2:20
I have been crucified with Christ and I no longer _____, but Christ _____ in me. The life I live in the body, I live by faith in the Son of God, who loved me and gave himself for me.

Romans 14:8
If we live, we _____ to the Lord; and if we_____, we die to the Lord. So, whether we live or die, we belong to the Lord.

2 Corinthians 5:15
And he _____ for all, that those who live should no longer live for themselves but for him who _____ for them and was raised again.

Looking Deeper

Discuss some of the things we may have to give up when we commit our lives to Christ. List a few of them below.

_____

_____

_____

_____

Compare your list to these possibilities:

- Doing whatever we want without considering what God wants.
- Friends who don't understand our commitment to God.
- Activities that don't please God.

Discuss some of the ways we can stand up for Christ in our modern world. List them below.

_____

_____

_____

_____

_____

_____

_____

Compare your list to these possibilities:

- Keeping our thoughts, words, and actions pleasing to God.
- Standing up for what is right.
- Telling others of our commitment to Christ.

For Mom:

Discuss with your daughter and then list below what has helped you gain courage to stand up for your commitment to Christ.

_____

_____

_____

_____

_____

_____

Discuss and identify three God-given qualities your daughter possesses that will help her face these challenges. Write them below.

1. _____

2. _____

3. _____

How can she use these qualities on a daily basis?

_____

_____

_____

For Discussion:

Discuss your ideas and list three things you can do this week to demonstrate your commitment to Christ.

1. _____

2. _____

3. _____

Action Ideas

Interview a grandmother, aunt, or an older woman in your church. You make up the questions! This can make for a fun and educational time. You could also make a dessert to share.

Words to Memorize

For to me, to live is Christ and to die is gain.
Philippians 1:21

Your Goal for This Week

_____

_____

_____

Closing Prayer

Lord, lead me toward a total commitment to You.

Week Fifteen

YOUR LIFE OR GOD'S

Scripture Reading for This Week

Psalm 40:5
Many, O Lord my God, are the wonders you have done. The things you planned for us no one can recount to you; were I to speak and tell of them, they would be too many to declare.

Psalm 145:13–20
Your kingdom is an everlasting kingdom, and your dominion endures through all generations. The Lord is faithful to all his promises and loving toward all he has made. The Lord upholds all those who fall and lifts up all who are bowed down. The eyes of all look to you, and you give them their food at the proper time. You open your hand and satisfy the desires of every living thing. The Lord is righteous in all his ways and loving toward all he has made. The Lord is near to all who call on him, to all who call on him in truth. He fulfills the desires of those who fear him; he hears their cry and saves them. The Lord watches over all who love him.

What words best describe the main point of these verses? Write them in the space below.

*Daughter*_____

Mom _____

Tell each other why you chose these words.

*H*annah struggled many years with her self-worth as a woman and as a wife because she was unable to have children. From her very early years, all that she ever wanted was to be a mother. Because of her inability to have children, she was considered a failure in her society. It was embarrassing for her husband, Elkanah, who loved her but could not comfort her.

Hannah did not know at that time, but all of this was in God's plan for her life. Hannah did not give up on her dream of becoming a mother, although she was sometimes discouraged about her situation. Her husband made sure she had a lot of good food, but she was too sad to eat it. She took her problem to God; she cried and prayed to Him. In fact, the Bible tells us that she was so distressed when she prayed that the priest thought she was drunk. She promised God if He would give her a child, she would give that child back to God. And when she finished praying, she was no longer sad, because she trusted that God would do the right thing. She really did want what God had planned for her life, not her own plan.

God answered Hannah's prayer and gave her a son. She named him Samuel. Even though it must have been a difficult promise for her to keep because she had wanted children so badly, Hannah remembered her promise to give her son to the Lord. So she took Samuel to the tabernacle to live with Eli, the priest. Each year his mother sewed him a coat and brought it to him. It probably made her sad sometimes when she had to leave him, but mostly she was happy that her son could serve God even when he was just a little boy. Hannah's willingness to give up the most important thing in her life served God also. Because she loved God so much she was willing to give Him the son she wanted more than anything, Hannah was later blessed with five more children.

And when Hannah's son Samuel grew up, he became one of Israel's greatest prophets. Hannah dreamed only of being a mother, but God planned for her to be the mother of one of the greatest leaders in Israel.

What the Story Says
Our best dreams can't compare to what God has planned for our lives.

Discussion Questions

1. How did Hannah ask God to make her dream come true?
2. Why do you think God answered Hannah's prayer? Was her answer worth waiting for?
3. When do you find it difficult to wait for an answer to prayer?

DEFINITION OF DREAM:
   A desire or hope; a wish or ambition; to imagine.

What Does the Bible Say?

Look up the following Scriptures and fill in the blanks.

Deuteronomy 30:20
And that you may_____ the Lord your God, _____ to his voice, and _____ to him. For the Lord is your _____, and he will give you many years in the land he swore to give to your fathers, Abraham, Isaac and Jacob.

How can we listen to God's voice?
What does it mean to "hold fast" to Him?

Matthew 10:39
Whoever _____ his life will lose it, and whoever _____ his life for my sake will find it.

What does it mean to lose your life?

Proverbs 3:5–6
Trust in the Lord with all your _____ and lean not on your _____ understanding; in all your ways acknowledge _____, and he will make your paths straight.

How can we avoid leaning on our own understanding?
How do we acknowledge Him?

Psalm 37:3–5
Trust in the Lord and do _____; dwell in the land and enjoy safe pasture. _____ yourself in the Lord and he will give you the desires of your heart. _____ your way to the Lord; trust in him.

What does it mean to do good?

What does it mean to delight yourself in the Lord?

John 10:10
The thief comes only to steal and kill and destroy; I have come
that they may have_____, and have it to the _____.

Who offers us a full life?

Colossians 1:10
And we pray this in order that you may live a life _____
of the Lord and may _____ him in every way.

Galatians 2:20
I have been _____ with Christ and I no
longer live, but Christ lives in me. The life I live in the body, I live
by _____ in the Son of God, who loved me and gave
himself for me.

Does Christ live in you?

1 Corinthians 6:20
You were_____ at a price. Therefore honor God
with your _____.

What does it mean to be "bought at a price"?

Word Scramble

1. turts _____
2. elgtdhi _____
3. tbuhog _____

(For answers, see page 196.)

Looking Deeper

How can we know what God wants for our lives? Discuss, then list some of your ideas below.

_____

_____

_____

_____

_____

Discuss some of the ways you can actively seek God's plan for your life. List them below.

_____

_____

_____

_____

_____

_____

Compare your list to these possibilities:

- Each morning, give your day to God in a brief prayer.
- Throughout the day, listen for God to speak to you.
- Watch for ways God is working in your life.

What can you do to prepare yourself to follow God's plan for your life? Discuss, then list a few of your ideas.

_____

_____

_____

_____

_____

_____

Compare your list to these ideas:

- Notice the opportunities God offers you each day.
- Read and study your Bible to see what God has to say to you each day.
- Memorize God's great promises.

For Mom:

Discuss the gifts God has given your daughter. What are her strengths and talents? Write them below.

_____

_____

_____

_____

_____

How might God use these special gifts for His purpose?

_____

_____

_____

_____

For Daughter:

What can you do to exercise these qualities on a daily basis? Ask your mom for some ideas also.

_____

_____

_____

_____

_____

_____

Super! Now you have a plan. Try practicing it this week.

For Discussion:

Discuss and list three ways that God can reveal His plan to you.

1. _____

2. _____

3. _____

Compare your list to this one:

- Through His Word.
- During your prayer time.
- In the opportunities He sends your way.

Action Ideas

Make (together) a meal for someone who has been ill or for someone who has just had a baby.

For Daughter:

Buy or make a nice card for your mother telling her what you really like about her, why you're glad she's your mother, and what you'll remember most about meeting together the last several weeks. Give it to her next week when you meet together.

Words to Memorize

Do not be afraid, little flock, for your Father
has been pleased to give you the kingdom.
Luke 12:32

Your Goal for This Week

_____

_____

_____

Closing Prayer

Lord, my life is not my own. It belongs to You. Guide me toward Your perfect plan.

Week Sixteen

A GIFT FROM
MOM'S HEART

---

om and daughter, this week is your chance to personalize your time together. First of all, Mom, you'll start by telling your daughter a story of your own. It could be how you came to know Christ. It could be the story of how you met and fell in love with your husband or the day your daughter was born.

Stop and ask yourself what is the one thing you want your daughter to know that was not covered so far in this book. If you could tell her only one thing, what would it be?

This is your chapter.

We have provided a space for you to write this story as a gift of love for your daughter. Don't worry, it's not really important if it's well written—the main thing is that the story you tell is personal. One day your daughter will treasure this simple and meaningful portrait of her family.

Ahead of time, write the story in the book. Then when you meet, begin by reading it aloud to her. You may prefer to "wing it" and tell your story impromptu. . . . Do what makes you feel the most comfortable. But be sure you write it down at some point so she'll have something to reread.

Then during the discussion phase of your time together, develop your own discussion questions and share favorite Scripture verses.

This is a gift of love to your daughter. So, get ready to tear off a piece of your heart and share it with her.

_____

_____

_____

_____

_____

_____

_____

_____

_____

_____

_____

_____

_____

_____

_____

_____

_____

_____

_____

_____

_____

_____

_____

_____

_____

_____

_____

_____

_____

_____

_____

_____

_____

_____

_____

_____

_____

_____

_____

_____

_____

_____

_____
_____
_____
_____
_____
_____
_____
_____
_____
_____
_____
_____
_____
_____
_____
_____
_____
_____
_____
_____
_____
_____
_____
_____
_____

What Your Story Says

_____

_____

_____

Discussion Questions

1. _____

2. _____

3. _____

For Mom:

Share your favorite Scripture passages. List the references below, then help your daughter look them up and ask her to read them.

_____

_____

_____

_____

_____

_____

Looking Deeper

Tell your daughter what you would like her to remember most about this story. Then write it below.

_____

_____

_____

_____

_____

_____

_____

_____

_____

_____

_____

Action Ideas

For Mom:

This is your week, Mom. Maybe you could plan a nice candle-light dinner in your dining room (use your china) for just you and your daughter. You may want to plan a dinner out at a nice restaurant—make it a special evening together. You could also have flowers delivered to your house for your daughter from you.

Words to Memorize

Your favorite memory verses:

*Mom*_____

_____

_____

_____

Daughter _____

_____

_____

_____

Your Goals for This Week

*Mom*_____

_____

_____

_____

_____

_____

_____

_____

Daughter _____

_____

_____

_____

_____

_____

_____

_____

_____

_____

Write a Closing Prayer

_____

_____

_____

_____

_____

_____

_____

_____

_____

_____

_____

_____

_____

_____

Benediction

But grow in the grace and knowledge of our Lord and
Savior Jesus Christ. To him be glory both now and forever!
Amen.

2 Peter 3:18

Answers to Word Scrambles:

Page 37
1. renew
2. purity
3. steadfast

Page 71
1. power
2. grace
3. knowledge

Page 123
1. confess
2. humble
3. forgiveness

Page 181
1. trust
2. delight
3. bought

Certificate of Completion

This is to certify that _____ and
_____ have together completed
the course of study in *Growing Little Women* on this
_____ day of _____, _____.

Signatures _____

_____

Certificate of Commitment

$\mathcal{T}$his is to certify that _____
and _____ have on this _____
day of _____, _____,
agreed to _____
_____.

Signatures _____

_____